GW00494280

THE MONEYMAKERS
international

W. Kranister

THE MONEYMAKERS
international

BLACK BEAR
PUBLISHING

Acknowledgements

Many friends and associates have helped to develop and edit this book.

Who they are — Where they are

Australia	Donald B. Addison, General Manager, Reserve Bank of Australia, Note Printing Branch
	R. G. Pearson, Marketing Manager, Reserve Bank of Australia, Note Printing Branch
	A. L. Flint, Curator, Reserve Bank of Australia, Note Printing Branch
Austria	Oesterreichische Nationalbank, Vienna:
	Herbert Skarke, Director
	Wolfgang Färber, Technical Manager
	Alfred Scherz
	Heinz Balzer
	Leopoldine Lechner
	Elisabeth Minichsdorfer
	Georg Leutner
	Peter Buchegger
	Robert Kalina
	Henry Wallner
	Elfriede Köllner
	Irene Sperl-Mühldorf
	Thomas Bartsch
China	Yin Yi, Director, Chinese Numismatic Society
England	Alex Jarvis, General Manager, Bank of England Printing Works
	Robin Baker, Bank of England Printing Works
	John Sidaway, Sales Director, Black Bear Press Limited
	John Keyworth, Curator of the Bank of England Museum
	Dr Jean McQueen, First Edition, Cambridge
Federal Republic of Germany	Hans Georg Emde, Mitglied des Direktoriums der Deutschen Bundesbank (retired)
	Günter Storch, Mitglied des Direktoriums der Deutschen Bundesbank
	Peter Titzhoff, Vizepräsident der Landeszentralbank Schleswig-Holstein
	Werner Meier, Bundesbankdirektor
	Walter Kolb, Geldmuseum der Deutschen Bundesbank
Spain	Jesus Urdiola, Chief Cashier, Banco de España
	Roberto Andrade, Advisor Engineer, Banco de España
Sweden	Sven Gideon, Vice President, AB Tumba Bruk (retired)
	Torgny Lindgren, author
	Ian Wisehn, Deputy Keeper at the Royal Coin Cabinet
United States of America	Gene Hessler, Curator
	Robert J. Leuver, Executive Director, American Numismatic Association, former Director of the Bureau of Engraving and Printing
	Peter H. Daly, Director, Bureau of Engraving and Printing
	Robin J. Kline, Bureau of Engraving and Printing
	Theodore Allison, Staff Director, Board of Governors of the Federal Reserve System
	Robert R. Snow, U.S. Secret Service
	Jane Vezeris, U.S. Secret Service

CONTENTS

INTRODUCTION

Instead of a conventional Preface, I should like to thank here everyone who has helped to make the production of this book possible.

The original idea of publishing "Moneymakers International" came about in a rather unusual way. I was talking to my good friend Bob Leuver, the former director of the Bureau of Engraving and Printing, when visiting Washington DC to publicise my Austrian book, *The Moneymakers – from the Gulden to the Schilling*. Bob was very enthusiastic about the book and suggested translating it into English and offering it for sale in the United States.

"Bob, that's a wonderful idea," I said, "but don't you think such a book might be more interesting if the chapters on Austria were shortened and milestones and highlights of some major countries were presented in addition? An international presentation might be better." So, some unintentional brainstorming occurred – and the idea of "Moneymakers International" was born.

That was in the autumn of 1985. Since then, a number of years of hard, but rewarding work have passed. It was hard because the book had to be assembled in addition to my quite intense and fascinating work as a member of the Austrian National Bank's Board of Executive Directors. It was rewarding because there were so many indications that enthusiasm and cooperation spanned four continents. There is one thing of which I am completely convinced: such a book could never have been developed if friends from eight countries on four continents had not co-operated on a project which has been based on significant mutual trust. The fact that this book has been produced at the same time in Chinese, English and German languages is a joy to both my friends and myself.

W. Kranister, Editor

THE BIRTH OF A BANKNOTE

Robert Kalina at work

Design

A top banknote designer is a gifted craftsman who can follow precise specifications to produce attractive notes that are difficult if not impossible to counterfeit. The latest security techniques must be – literally – at his fingertips, for forgery is a constant threat to banknote producers, and a design's beauty may not offer it any protection. An artist designer must be able to exploit the possibilities of all the available printing techniques – some of them novel and exciting – and usually works full-time for one notemaking company.

Robert Kalina's rough sketches for a new Austrian note

The banknote first sees the light of day in the form of a portfolio of pencil sketches suggesting ways of combining the essential details of the design: the value of the note and several graphic elements – lettering, line decorations (guilloches), often one or more portraits, perhaps a landscape.

The choice of the graphic elements often follows traditional lines. Portraits and figure drawings are common; U.S. bills for instance, have carried the likenesses of American statesmen since the nineteenth century, while Bank of England notes, once ruled by Britannia alone, have included the portrait of Queen Elizabeth II since the 1950s. Landscape and architectural motifs often appear on the backs of notes. Guilloches – intricate geometric patterns of interwoven wavy lines – have decorated banknotes at least since the beginning of the last century.

The most suitable sketches for the two sides of the banknote are chosen from the designer's portfolio. From these the prototype note is drawn and coloured. The prototypes look exactly like finished banknotes, perfect in every detail – they are works of art in themselves. It usually takes the artist and his team about six months to design one side of a banknote; an especially complicated design may take longer.

A design showing an Austrian landscape drawn by Josef Seger

10

Making masters for dry offset printing

The different elements of prototype design are often printed by different techniques. For example, the graphic features are usually printed by the intaglio method, which produces an extremely sharp image, while the background designs and the security grid are printed by the dry offset process (U.S. bills have no background print). Sometimes the whole of the reverse of low-denomination notes is printed in dry offset, for economy's sake.

The first step in preparing the plates for dry offset printing is therefore to separate the design elements from each other. Often a computer-aided method is used. Next the background designs for both the front and back of the note are separated into up to four parts each, which will be printed separately but simultaneously. A "master" – a special plastic film – is then prepared from each part and the printing plates are manufactured from these films, usually by an elaborate multi-stage process. In the Orloff process, however, the background designs are printed in a single pass, thus achieving perfect registration (that is, exact alignment of the design elements). Chinese banknotes are printed using an advanced technique of this kind.

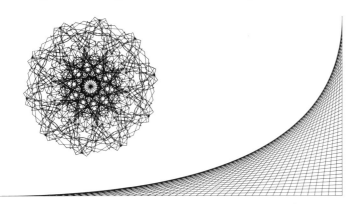

Background motif for dry offset printing, on the screen of the computer guilloche machine (CADCAM method)

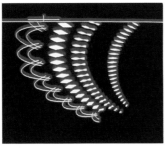

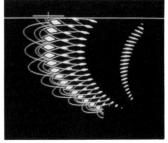

Making dies for intaglio printing

Intaglio printing uses highly polished copper or steel plates or dies, into which the design is cut. This is where the engraver's task begins: it requires artistic flair combined with extreme precision and accuracy. His starting-point is the engraver's model, which is specially prepared from the prototype drawing. He reproduces each feature of the model as a system of fine lines and dots, which he cuts into the die at varying depths and angles. As he works he prepares trial prints of the intermediate stages, so that he can monitor the progress of the die and refine its detail. Prints of the engraved die ("engravings") have a characteristic three-dimensional look produced by raised lines and dots of ink. This texture cannot be reproduced photographically, so it is a useful deterrent to the counterfeiter.

Master drawing, and the engraving made from it

Once the engraver is satisfied with the trial proofs he passes the die to the guilloche-maker, who transfers the guilloches onto the plate using a guilloche machine, which scratches away a special protective coating with either a steel or a diamond stylus. Often the note's denomination and lettering are added, and finally the die is etched, that is, it is treated with acid, which bites into the metal surface where it has been exposed by the removal of the protective coating. The etcher's task is difficult and delicate; he could ruin months of the engraver's work by a moment's carelessness.

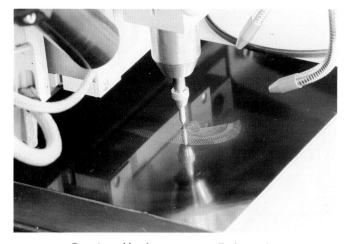

Drawing table of a computer guilloche machine

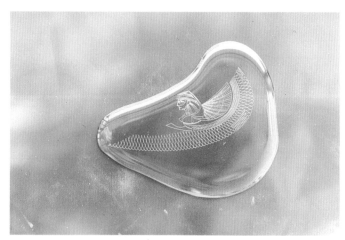

Etching a guilloche pattern

Proof prints

Proofs of both the background design and of the intaglio-printed material can now be struck, and any faults corrected. At this point the inks for the final printing are chosen, with careful matching to the colours of the prototype design. Mixtures of inks are used rather than single inks, so as to make counterfeiting even more difficult to carry out and easier to detect.

Making the plates

Now the production of the printing plates can begin. All the plates carry a grid of identical images, so that a large number of notes are printed at once.

The dry offset process uses two kinds of plate: some are copper or brass, with the design etched onto their surface, while others are plastic-coated steel, produced by exposing sensitised plates in a flatbed scanner. The chromium-coated nickel plates for intaglio printing are made electrolytically, however, using the electrotype process. Each plate is examined, millimetre by millimetre, to detect and put right any flaws.

Final retouching of the plate

Paper

Banknotes are always printed on high-quality paper. Usually it is cotton-based, and contains characteristic threads, fibres and watermarks to make it easily identifiable and difficult to imitate. The exact properties of the raw materials for its production, as well as those of the finished paper itself, are agreed by the banknote producer and the paper manufacturer.

Wax engraving the original of a watermark

Feeding the security thread into the wet pulp

Formation of the watermark

Sheet printing

Sheets of banknotes are produced by a sequence of printing processes. First the paper sheets are run through simultaneous printing presses, which print the background designs of the front and back of each note with eight different printing units at once (four for each side). The registration in this process is precise to about a hundredth of a millimetre – that is, perfect to the naked eye.

Transparent register ornament:

front   *view (through)*   *back*

Next comes the intaglio printing of the pictorial features, the guilloches and the lettering. The cylinder of an intaglio press carries up to four printing units. First the grooves of the plates are loaded with ink; then the paper is pressed onto the plate with great force. Under this pressure – up to 100 tons – the ink is lifted from the grooves in the plate and sticks to the paper. The ridges of ink thus formed on a banknote's surface can easily be felt; their presence accounts for the way in which some banknotes change their appearance when light falls on them at varying angles. This "tilting effect" is clearly seen beside the portraits on current Austrian banknotes.

Details of intaglio printing

Tilting effect

ink

paper

plate

Lastly, the sheets pass through numbering presses, which use the letterpress technique to stamp each note with its alphanumeric "number".

Web Printing

Instead of printing pre-cut paper sheets by several different processes, some banknote producers use a single large press continuously fed from reels of uncut paper. Within the machine the paper passes in turn through dry offset, intaglio and numbering presses; the order of the units varies from one works to another.

Web printing is used mainly in Great Britain, Denmark, Finland and Sweden. Whether its results are better than those of sheet printing is arguable. Each manufacturer naturally finds the virtues of his system self-evident, so the debate is likely to continue.

Electronic controls ensure precision in cutting and delivery

The paper moves at 120m/min (390ft/min)

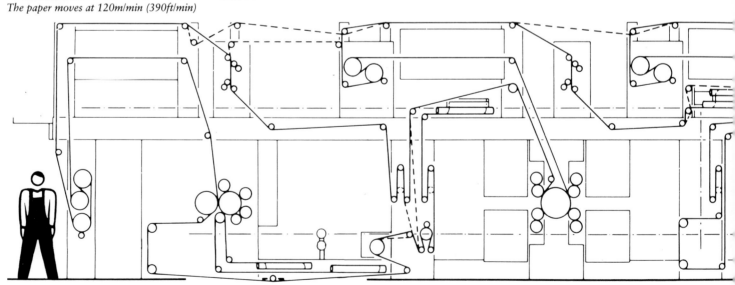

Finishing

Finally, every banknote must pass a quality control inspection before it is issued. Any defective notes are rejected and destroyed at this stage. The finished notes are cut, sorted, counted and packed, in some works by fully automated note processing machinery.

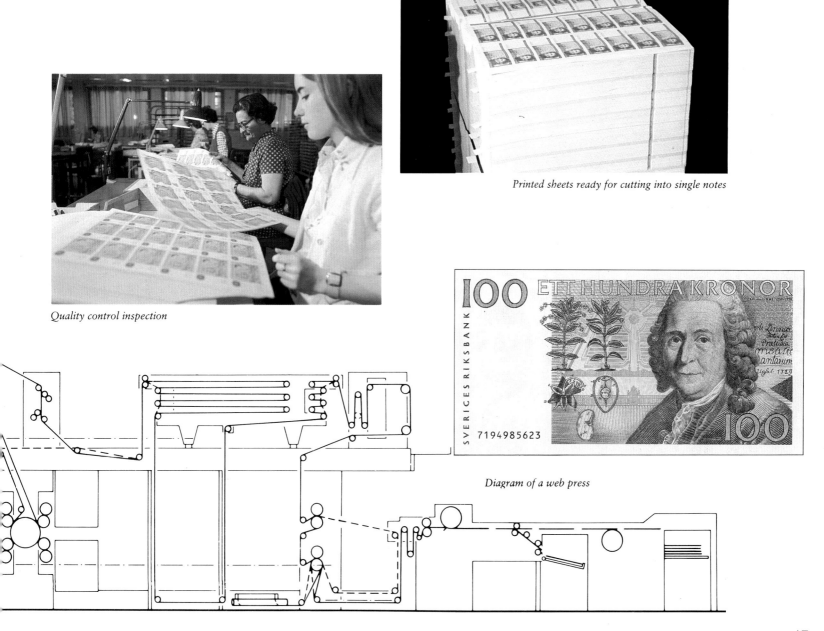

Printed sheets ready for cutting into single notes

Quality control inspection

Diagram of a web press

THE PHILOSOPHY OF BANKNOTE PRINTING

The first western banknotes were simple. Some were even handwritten; others were printed by letterpress using the basic printing materials available in every composing room. Precautions against counterfeiting, however, soon became necessary, and the process became more sophisticated. Die stamped personal wax seals and seals of the issuing bank were used at first, and later decorative borders and other ornamentation were introduced. Specially cut typefaces were produced for some notes. Stereotypes, electrotypes and steel printing units were also used in order to provide more stable and durable printing material. Watermarked paper was introduced; the first Swedish banknote to have a specific watermark was issued in 1666 by the Stockholm Bank. The philosophy of banknote printing had already crystallised to include as many unique processes and features as possible.

Letterpress printed image

Security features

By the end of the nineteenth century, two distinct schools of Banknote manufacture had evolved, one in Europe and the other in the U.S.A.

Most European-style notes have watermarked paper, often with a multitone watermark, intaglio printing and background patterns produced in multicolour letterpress or lithograph. Sometimes scattered coloured fibres or bands of coloured fibres are introduced into the paper.

Multi-colour intaglio print

By contrast, American-style notes have no watermark, but the paper contains coloured fibres, planchettes or a security thread. Most use only intaglio printing, and it is not secured by background printing in letterpress or lithograph. Up to the middle of the twentieth century, single-colour intaglio printing was normally used on both European and U.S. banknotes, but European banknotes then began to appear in multicolour intaglio with dry offset background tints. American banknotes continue to use single-colour intaglio printing, though sometimes background tints are used.

In the Third World both types of banknotes appear, depending on their place of manufacture.

Watermark "Anton Bruckner"

19

The Soviet Union and some middle European countries have used (and are still using) the Orloff process, in which the printing unit creates lines with changing colours. This kind of print is extremely difficult to reproduce.

Ever since banknotes were first issued, banks have tried to protect their notes from counterfeiters by using unique methods of printing (such as intaglio) and by including features that are not commercially available. But the recent rapid progress in reproduction techniques and the intensive marketing of scanners and colour copiers have made further precautions necessary. Holograms and kinegrams, security features that can easily be recognised by the public, have been discussed but until now their use has been limited by their very high cost.

Design features can, however, be incorporated to make banknotes harder to reproduce using scanners and colour copiers. Some of the new automatic note-processing machines can also check authenticity, and this has allowed the introduction of novel security features – into the security thread, the paper or the ink – of which the public is quite unaware.

Even more than professional forgers, banknote printers maintain a constant watch for opportunities for counterfeiting their notes, for they are well aware not only that most people accept a banknote as genuine without a second glance, but also of the heavy responsibility they carry to produce documents that are as secure as possible.

Orloff print

The last century has seen the transformation of banknote printing from a small-scale operation on hand-fed flatbed presses into mass production using highly sophisticated printing equipment. Multicolour intaglio printing has been used increasingly in the last forty years, and since 1970 web printing has been adopted by some countries for most of their production.

Web printing offers many production advantages. Banknotes are printed from a roll of watermarked paper and converted into finished banknotes in a single process, minimising security control costs and giving a more consistent product quality. Some recently developed systems can convert the printed rolls (after a visual inspection) into finished, counted banknote bundles ready for issue. Within the next few years web presses will include automatic colour control, automatic quality inspection and the marking of spoiled notes on-line, enabling notes to be sorted automatically on- or off-line.

Today's banknote is an industrial product, manufactured at a cost related to the required level of security and standard of printing. Normal cost–risk relations may not be applied; security must always be the overriding consideration.

THE ART OF DESIGNING AND ENGRAVING BANKNOTES

As we have seen, producing a banknote is a highly technical process, in which the manufacturers are constrained by all kinds of pressures and limitations and the product has to be made in enormous numbers, perhaps reaching virtually every household in the country. But every note begins its life at the end of the pencil of a single gifted individual, the artist designer.

   We interviewed one such man: Harry Eccleston, of the Bank of England Printing Works.

Harry Eccleston – bank note design artist

Do you recall, Harry, how things were before you joined the Printing Works?

Back in the 1950s Bank of England notes were designed by professional artists, each note design contract being awarded following a design competition; for example, Stone and Austin designed all the Series C notes between them.

And all that changed when the Bank recruited you in January 1958?

No, not straight away. At the start I worked only on experimental designs. David Wicks had joined the Printing Works as an artist/engraver some years earlier, initially on a part-time basis, and he and I acted as assistants to Professor Austin, the Bank's consultant designer. It was several years before I was trusted to design a proper banknote.

So when did the great British public first handle one of your own designs?

In 1970 – it was the £20 Series D note. I know that sounds ridiculous, as if it took me years to convince people here that I was up to the job! But it wasn't like that – honestly. Let me explain. I worked on a new ten-shilling note

Reverse of 50p coin

Front of the unissued ten-shilling Series D note

Back of the unissued ten-shilling Series D note

Master drawing of Sir Walter Raleigh

which it was planned would be the first of Series D: it was a beautiful note to design – all offset in various shades of brown and orange, with Sir Walter Raleigh as the historical figure on the reverse. It was designed to be printed on our new Simultan presses and was also unique because we were due to go over to decimal currency and the design had to be adaptable to read either "Fifty new pence" or "Ten shillings". But in 1964, when the design was approved and production was just getting under way, the Government decided to bring out the fifty-pence coin instead: so my first English banknote was stillborn, although I had earlier designed some notes for Singapore which Bradbury Wilkinson engraved and printed.

How strange – so the Royal Mint scuppered your first note before you could launch it, and sank your £1 note as well soon after you retired. And both coins are still going strong!

I must say I like your naval metaphor. Seriously, though, I'm sure you'll agree that the notes are far better works of art.

No question of that, Harry. Now tell me a little about your early career.

Well, I studied at art college in Birmingham until 1942. Interestingly, Birmingham was one of the few places in the U.K. where portrait drawing was taught. Then I spent four years in the Royal Navy and didn't get much opportunity for painting more than the occasional bit of superstructure. When I left the service I went back to school – I was twenty-four by then – and studied under Professor Austin at the Royal College of Art, and I kept in touch with him after I left in 1951 to teach Illustration and Graphic Design at South-East Essex Technical College in Barking where I developed a great interest in typography. Whilst at Barking I started producing etched intaglio plates of industrial subjects – in fact, I still did until about a year ago. Professor Austin recruited me from Barking for the Printing Works.

So you really became a banknote artist by accident rather than by design?

Yes, I suppose so, although on reflection I can see that my training and experience at various stages combined to give me a very good understanding of the various basic aspects of banknote design. Of course, banknote design is totally different from any other art form.

Romeo and Juliet *(the balcony scene): vignette in gouache by Harry Eccleston for the reverse of the £20 Series D note*

Why is that?

Well, to start with it is the least "free" form – in other words, there is more limitation, more restriction on the artist's own freedom of expression. The "canvas" is ridiculously tiny, and there is no normal "frame" to your picture – the edge is more of a wavy line. Add to that all the words you are obliged to include for statutory purposes, and then the restrictions that printing from an engraved plate impose upon the monarch's portrait, which we have also to include – well, you see what I mean. And I haven't even mentioned the various different features one includes to try and make the forger's job more difficult, things like micro-lettering, machine engraving and hand engraving, close registered backgrounds, "white line" and "black line", vignettes, asymmetrically based patterns, to name but a few! On top of all that, the design has to be capable of mass reproduction on high-speed presses so that notes printed years apart look identical when placed side by side."

I agree – banknote design isn't an easy art form. One thing you didn't mention in that long list was the amount of historical research you have to do. What would you say is the balance between research and actual design?

About fifty-fifty. Take the £20 note, which has Shakespeare on it. Lots of material – I visited Stratford-on-Avon, I looked at prints and paintings, sketches and portraits; I read books about him; I even saw the odd Shakespeare play! In all, I spent perhaps three months on research, with another three months preparing the various master

drawings that made up the whole note. Although, of course, it doesn't work out as two separate periods of three months; you really can't separate research and design.

So, like a character actor playing a famous person, you try and get "inside" your subject?

Yes, exactly. But that doesn't mean that I visited Waterloo before designing the £5 note – although I

Harry Eccleston (left) with the Bank of England's current Artist Designer, Roger Withington, discussing a new note design

Roger Withington's pencil drawing of London and St Paul's for the £50 Series D note

25

Battle scene: master for the back of the £5 Series D note, painted in gouache by Harry Eccleston

did spend a lot of time in St Paul's Cathedral when the £50 note was on the drawing board. When Roger Withington [who succeeded Harry Eccleston as the Bank's artist designer] prepared the master drawing for the back of that note, he was up there for days.

But surely, Harry, that's a bit excessive – are you trying to tell me all this research is necessary?

I most certainly am. I can't over emphasise how important it is. Remember what you're designing: a banknote. Every single member of the public suddenly becomes an art critic! Take the £1 Newton note. We had letters from members of the Newton Society saying the eye-piece on the telescope was in the wrong place, and his coat buttons were the wrong style for the period! And for the £5 note I was told that I had drawn the wrong number of spokes on the wheel of the chariot.

Do you design a series of notes rather than just a lot of single denominations?

That's a good question. The short answer is yes – the artist is trying to do two things. First of all, each note should be a single, integrated design, not just a collection of different parts. I'm not being disrespectful to my predecessors, but look at Series C or B notes and then look at the present ones. What we have now is a blending together of several different designs into a single piece of artwork so that you can hardly tell, for example, where the geometric lathe work ends and the hand-engraving begins. In fact, this approach led us to make several interesting modifications to our Kampf lathe.

And we try and do that with all the notes in the series. So you use the same style of Queen's portrait on each note, each has an historical figure on the back – again a portrait – with a relevant scene illustrating the subject's achievements, and they all have the same look and balance so that anyone can tell at a glance that the £5 and £50 notes come from the same "family". It did seem to be important, however, that the character of the historical subject should influence the style of the design, and so on each note an appropriate form of lettering and pattern from the period was used.

Would you like to say a word or two about the other members of the design team?

I'm glad you used the word "team" because that is exactly what we are. A banknote is a combination of several different art forms. So you need different skills to produce the complete note: as well as the artist you need a lettering engraver, a portrait engraver, a geometric lathe expert, a lithographic artist – not to mention the printers and inkmakers. They may work in different parts of the organisation but they're still very much a part of the team.

Master drawings of the Queen's portrait for Series D notes

I suppose the artist designer's job is to conceive the whole note in outline form and then to discuss and develop different aspects with these various experts. Each, of course, is a skilled craftsman in his own right and he or she (none of our artists or engravers are women, but there are, I know, some quite excellent ones working for other countries) will have his own views and "interpretation" of his part of the overall design. But unless one person has the complete design in his mind's eye and can communicate this "vision" to the rest of the design team you'll end up with a collection of spare parts rather than a balanced note. I don't think I'm boasting when I say that the best answer to your question about the importance of team work is to look at our present notes. A first-class note will only be born if a first-class team conceives and delivers it!

One final question, Harry. There is no school for banknote artists, no degree or diploma in banknote design. So where would you go to find such a rare species?

It can be quite difficult. Artists are all different and all will have developed differently, even if they all came from the same art school. Creating a banknote is a living, dynamic process. It's really a kind of adult apprenticeship "learn as you go" – mine, as I mentioned earlier, lasted a number of years! But to try and answer your question: where to look? Well, you need someone with experience of graphic design, catholic tastes in art, skill in draughtsmanship, some knowledge of printing and lettering, but above all, genuine artistic talent. Each banknote is a piece of artwork – in fact, it's two if you turn it over and look at the back. It's not a filing cabinet or a bit of furniture, so it needs an artist/designer, not just a designer. But then you could say I was biased.

The caduceus vignette used on the front of the £1 Series D note

27

Maria Laurent, Banknote engraver

Many countries have a tradition of banknote production. This also applies to the use of copper engraving, whose origins date back to elaborately engraved helmets, armour and weapons of the Middle Ages. Ink probably got into the grooves by accident one day, prompting the discovery that very lovely prints could be made, although they were inverted. A fifteenth-century German goldsmith, known as the Master of Playing Cards after his most famous work, was one of the first people to make prints on paper from engraved plates. The golden age of copper engraving was initiated with the masterpieces of Albrecht Dürer; later, great painters like Raphael and Rubens, hoping to get wider recognition for their work, commissioned specialist studios to make copper engraving of their paintings, and thus pioneered the use of engraving for reproduction purposes.

Intaglio printed motifs

Copper engraving came into use for banknote printing because of its inimitability, a quality that every banknote manufacturer looks for. It was first used on a banknote in the Electorate of Saxony in 1772. Austrians adopted it for the first time to print Gulden notes in the nineteenth century. Ever since then, the main motifs have been copper-engraved and printed on the banknotes by the intaglio process; copper engraving has remained one of the principal security features of banknotes down to the present day.

But what does a copper engraver today actually do? To find out, we interviewed one of today's top banknote engravers, Maria Laurent of the Austrian National Bank.

Mrs Laurent, copper engraving is an unusual way of making a living, and you are one of a very few women in this line of work. How did you find your way into the profession, and where did you train?

I have loved drawing ever since I was a child and I passionately wanted to be a fashion designer. I was lucky enough to have a teacher who recognised that I had a talent for drawing and who encouraged me very much. The choice between a commercial school and an industrial school with a branch for metalwork, including engraving and metal embossing, was easy; my other ambitions turned into daughters.

After leaving school I engraved hunting guns for a Vienna firm, and when I heard that the Austrian National Bank was looking for an engraver, I applied for the job. I had the right background, but I still had to learn banknote engraving step by step, as it is completely different from any other kind of engraving, and Professor Nefe both taught me and supervised my studies.

Thanks to the generosity of our Bank, I also had the chance to study both at the Vienna Graphic Art School and at the Academy of the Applied Arts in Vienna, where I went to drawing classes held by Professor Ranzoni Jr and Professor Baszel.

What materials and tools do copper engravers use?

First I need a completely flat copper plate about 2 mm thick, meticulously polished. The main tools I use are the burin, a scraper and several magnifying glasses. Incidentally, the burin has not changed since the fifteenth century, and no one has managed to invent a tool that is more suitable.

Maria Laurent at work

Finished printing plate for the intaglio process

What does banknote engraving mean? How can engraving provide protection against counterfeiting?

Banknote engraving must allow for the special limitations of printing presses, which are different for every new generation of presses. Engraving is difficult to counterfeit because of its precision, the accuracy with which the lines are cut, the interaction of fine and bold lines and the combination of copper engraving and intaglio printing, all of which go together to produce the characteristic texture of the engraved note.

The banknote designer's maxim ('beauty is optional, security a necessity") is something that engravers naturally have to observe too.

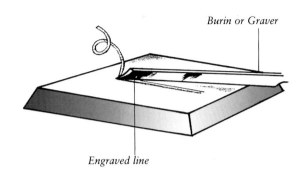

Burin or Graver

Engraved line

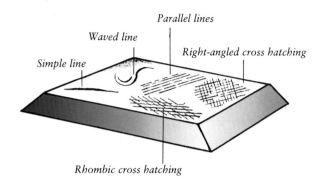

Parallel lines

Waved line

Right-angled cross hatching

Simple line

Rhombic cross hatching

Engraving techniques

How do you engrave a plate, and how long does it take? Can you add your own personal style to an engraving?

I use the burin to cut fine lines and dots into a copper plate. It takes me up to a year to complete a single plate, depending on the motif, of course. My individual style lies in the way I interpret the design, how I decide on the breadth of the lines and how to arrange them to produce the three-dimensional effect I want. Every engraver owns the copyright to his artwork, but banknote engravers assign their copyright to the central bank, of course.

This work certainly needs a controlled approach and a steady hand, since corrections are very difficult, if not impossible to make. How do you keep calm, and when do you not?

You really do need to be able to concentrate for this job. Corrections can be made, but they require a lot of time and effort. If I feel a bit on edge I leave the facial expression for instance, for a better day, and work on something like a wall instead. On a bad day, it's probably better for me not to touch the plate at all.

Don't you ever get bored with working on one and the same portrait for such a long time? Can you still look at this face after a year?

My first portrait was of the poet Grillparzer, who was a rather surly man. In the beginning, I saw only this bitterness in his face – but the more often I looked at it the more beautiful it became to me, and in the end I nearly fell in love with it. So I always look at people closely, and I find I can often discover the beauty that underlies the first superficial impression. I think this is something my trade has taught me, because when I engrave someone's portrait, and I want to convey his expression, I have to project myself into this person and analyse his character very intensely and thoroughly. I can't do this on the basis of a passing glance.

Maria Laurent's engraving of Franz Grillparzer

Carl Ritter von Ghega,
the builder of the Semmering railway

What was your first banknote? Have you engraved many banknotes, and what do you now think of your first engravings?

My first banknote was the twenty-Schilling note with the portrait of Ritter von Ghega, but since then I have engraved the motifs of a great many others. Looking back on my first efforts, I think I might have done some things differently if I had had more experience. But I have always tried to do my best. I do gain expertise from one banknote to the next, and I do use this knowledge – something that applies in every profession, I think. Just having talent is not enough; you have to work at it.

In your spare time you engrave postage stamps and you draw, you also have a family and run a home. How do you manage all this?

I need to draw to complement my work, but I have far too little time. As a banknote and stamp engraver with a family, household and friends, I have plenty to do – and personal activities are very important to me, too, so sometimes I get close to the limits of my capacity. I think men do have it easier in this respect. But after all, I do have a job that absorbs me, that lets me develop my artistic skills and that gives me a chance of personal growth. Besides, what other artist gets their work reproduced in such a huge edition that everyone can own it?

Stamp engraving
by Maria Laurent

TECHNICAL EQUIPMENT:
HIT PARADE OF INNOVATIONS

Ten-Reichsthaler Cassen-Billet of 1772 (detail)

GERMANY

Like all other banknotes, the German Reich's paper money incorporated safeguards against counterfeiting from the very beginning, both in banknote paper and in printed matter. Among the earliest of these safeguards was watermarking. The oldest watermark is found in Saxon notes issued in 1772, and showed writing. Image watermarks, such as the representation of the coat of arms on Schleswig-Holstein's bills of 1802 and the ornamental plant motif on Baden's first bills of 1849, were rare at first but became more common in the second half of the nineteenth century.

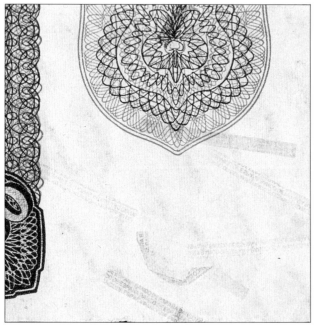

Giesecke & Devrient's patent banknote paper

Paper

Distinctive paper developed alongside watermarks. At the beginning of the 1880s, the Prussian National Printing Works purchased the right to use the paper developed by and named after its inventor, James Wilcox, in which coloured plant fibres were embedded. Counterfeiters tried to imitate these fibres by pasting human and brush hair onto their forged notes.

The company Giesecke & Devrient, founded in Leipzig in 1852, soon took the lead in the development of banknote paper in Germany. In 1906 the firm took out patents in Germany, England and Switzerland for the incorporation of strips of pre-printed paper of different colours, cut to the same length, into the wet paper web as a highly effective device against forgery, in addition to the watermark. A 1939 patent protected an improved version of this process, it allowed for printed metal pieces or planchettes to be embedded in the paper mass at the time of manufacture.

Printing

The early printing techniques used to deter forgers were unsophisticated. The individual German states favoured various methods: different types of writing (in Saxony and Meiningen), names and initials hidden in ornaments (in Pomerania and the Ducal State Bank of Nassau), relief printing (in Frankfurt and Saxony), embossing dies (in Erfurt and Baden – sometimes the dies were intentionally cracked) and the register printing of motifs on the fronts and backs of the notes (in Frankfurt and Baden). Basically, all forgery prevention methods relied on continuous paper, watermarks and constantly updated printing technology.

Security features used in the past

The Reich Printing Works

After the Reichsbank's foundation in 1876, the newly unified German monetary system needed its own central banknote printing works. The Reich Printing Works (Reichsdruckerei) was therefore set up in 1879, with twelve copperplate printing presses, twelve hand-operated letterpress printing machines and twenty-two high speed presses. The oldest press for banknote printing was the hand-operated copperplate press; it was manned by an inker, who inked the plate, and a printer, who wet-wiped the plate and positioned the sheet in line with the register markings for printing. The purchase of a dual hand press operated by two teams increased daily output to between 600 and 800 four-note sheets.

An increasing demand for banknotes required copperplate printing to be mechanised. New four-plate copperplate printing presses (Nadherny presses) were provided by the Vienna-based company of Carl Neuburger; their structure was similar to that of the Miehle four-plate press developed in Germany, except that the plates were inked and wiped automatically.

The next step forward in the automation of banknote printing is represented by the line printing press developed by the Reich Printing Works in co-operation with Koenig & Bauer of Würzburg. It included several fully automatic features: inking, plate wiping with a calico wiping system, sheet feeding and delivery. The most novel feature was the arrangement of the plates on a rotary cylinder. The press had an output of 5,000 to 6,000 sheets per eight hour shift and was used in the Federal Printing Works, the successor to the Reich Printing Works, from 1928 until its replacement by simultaneous printing presses in 1958.

Giesecke & Devrient

Most of the technical innovations in German banknote printing originated with the firm of Giesecke & Devrient. The company was entrusted with the production of the Royal Saxon lottery tickets in 1899, for which a specially manufactured, patented machine, was used to print the serial numbers on the fronts and backs of the tickets simultaneously. The same machine was later used to overprint numbers on currency notes.

An example of printed numbering by the Reich Printing Works

Giesecke & Devrient's headquarters moved from Leipzig to Munich in 1948. In order to continue banknote printing, the company set up a steel gravure sheet-fed rotary press in Lausanne four years later, in conjunction with the printing press manufacturer Koenig & Bauer and the Giori organisation. The press operated on the three-colour stencil cylinder principle, with a wiping cylinder replacing conventional paper or calico wiping.

Three-colour intaglio printing press

Giesecke & Devrient's first simultaneous printing press for indirect letterpress printing came into operation in 1957. It was capable of simultaneous three-plate printing of note faces and two-plate printing of note backs. In co-operation with the manufacturers of etching machines, a process was developed to permit the use of continuously etched zinc plates in this type of press for the first time. In 1958, together with Faber & Schleicher, the firm also developed the first indirect letterpress printing machine (dry offset) to print banknote and security backgrounds.

Automatic banknote processing

The Automation and Organisation Company (GAO), established in 1970, was asked by the Bundesbank two years later to develop a system to process paper money automatically at the German Central Bank and to build the machines required for this purpose. Production of the first notes suitable for automatic processing began in 1975. These notes were encoded with invisible machine-identifiable and machine-readable information, so that they could automatically be checked for genuineness and their value identified. The system has now been introduced in many other central banks.

A modern ISS 300 note-processing machine was delivered to the Bundesbank in 1977. This fully automated machine, which handles between four and eight banknotes a second, inspects the condition of banknotes returned from circulation, as well as verifying their authenticity and value.

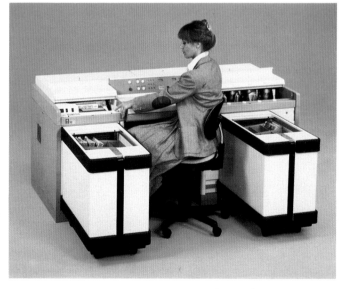

Fully automatic note-processing machines

SWEDEN

Guilloche patterns by C. A. Broling

In 1829, C A Broling, who was employed at the Swedish Royal Mint, unveiled a geometric lathe which he had developed for creating guilloches and, as a result, the Central Bank decided to use this type of security pattern on its next series of banknotes for the first time. Few details of the lathe's mechanism survive and we have only a vague idea what it looked like, but the specimen illustrated above shows its capabilities. Other geometric lathes were developed in several European countries and in the United States during the first half of the nineteenth century.

In 1905 it was decided to improve the security of Swedish banknotes by introducing a three-colour background print using letterpress, and a new press was designed for this purpose at the Bank of Sweden's Banknote Printing Works. It was a flatbed press with three inking units and a revolving triangular device supporting the printing units which were automatically inked with three different colours. The printing was carried out on wet banknote paper and the machine was hand-fed.

In 1950, a patent was granted for a paper counting machine invented by Axel Rosswall, who was the Banknote Printing Works' technical manager. Rosswall tried to get his machine made in Sweden, but no Swedish company was interested because the market was thought to be too small. The patent was therefore sold to Portals in England who formed a new company, Vacuumatic, for manufacturing the equipment.

Three-colour letterpress

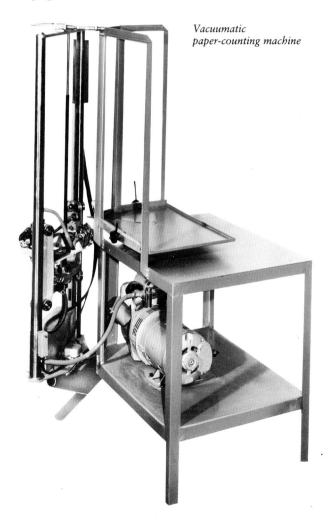

*Vacuumatic
paper-counting machine*

During the 1950s Rosswall, together with Peter Price from the Bank of England Printing Works, started to look into the possibility of using web printing for banknotes. In the next few years a test machine was made: the intaglio unit was manufactured by Goebel in Darmstadt and the offset unit by Victory Kidder in England. This test press produced the first web-printed banknotes; some indeed were issued.

In 1958 the Bank of Sweden decided to buy a web press from Goebel and this started to print five-kronor banknotes in 1961. The operating sequence on this machine was interesting in itself. First, a dry offset two-colour front and two-colour back was produced in a simultaneous printing unit using heat-set inks and open gas driers for drying the ink. There followed a single-colour intaglio unit in which the wiping of the intaglio was carried out with a paper wiping unit assisted by an ink recovery band, and the intaglio ink was dried with open flame gas driers. Then came numbering and cutting into sheets. This press operated until 1986, much of the time using a two shift manning system.

Goebel web press, installed in 1961

Web press for multicolour dry offset and intaglio printing, installed in 1980

Encouraged on by the success in web printing, the bank bought a new web press in 1978. The best tender was put in by the Finnish firm Wartsila, and the new press has been printing both Swedish and foreign banknotes since 1980.

The limited number of offset colours in the old Goebel press were considered to be inadequate, so the specification for the new equipment included a capability for four-colour printing of both the fronts and the backs of notes, together with multicolour intaglio printing with paper wiping. The intaglio unit is placed first in the printing sequence, so as to have the paper in the best possible condition for this process. Intaglio can be printed on both sides in two passes: the back is printed in the first pass and the paper is then re-reeled ready for the second. There is a pre-wiping unit, for improved inking and wiping, and both the intaglio and the dry offset prints are dried with open-flame gas driers. Two separate offset units, built on the satellite principle, print the fronts and backs of notes; however, the press can achieve a print register very close to that of the old simultaneous press, and

Dry offset printing unit

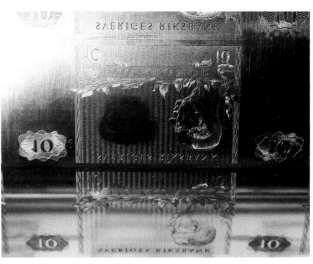

A hard-chromed intaglio plate

Watermarked banknote paper

Numbering boxes

can even print transparent register, while watermarks can be registered at a closer tolerance than for sheet-fed machines. Notes can be numbered on the front only or on both front and back in the press, which delivers finished banknote sheets.

This equipment is a major step towards more cost-effective large-scale production of banknotes, as well as for lesser quantities of 20 to 30 million notes. The manufacturing rights are now held by the German company Miller-Johannisberg.

AB TUMBA BRUK

ENGLAND

Banknote threads

In the early 1930s Stanley Chamberlain, the General Manager of the Bank of England Printing Works, in co-operation with Portals Ltd, began experimenting with various ways of embedding a thread in a banknote. Threads had been used in other documents before, but not in papers that had to withstand the rough treatment met with by banknotes. Such a thread needs to be flexible enough to avoid causing local defects that might lead to tearing. It has to be compatible with modern, high speed papermaking machinery so that it does not affect the machine's ability to produce large quantities of high-quality paper. Above all, the public must be able to identify it easily. Chamberlain's work led to the invention of the metallic security thread, which he patented in 1935, a second patent being granted in 1938 to cover some modifications.

The first note to include this type of thread was the £1 note issued by the Bank of England on 29 March 1940. Since then the Chamberlain thread has been used in most of the Bank's notes, and indeed in those of many other issuing authorities. It was not until over forty years later that a banknote was issued with a significantly different thread. This was the £50 note issued on 20 March 1981, in which one edge of the security thread was contoured rather than straight. This thread was produced on equipment jointly developed by the Bank of England Printing Works and the U.K. Atomic Energy Authority, in which the programmed oscillation of a laser beam produced the contoured edge.

For some years, issuing authorities have watched with considerable anxiety the development of high-quality, low-cost colour copier machines. Their threat was met by the Bank of England Printing Works in 1984 by a modified Chamberlain thread that surfaced at regular intervals. When banknotes that have this feature are photocopied, the exposed metallic strip comes out as a black dotted line which the public can identify at a glance. Once again, there was very close co-operation with Portals to perfect a method for producing paper with this type of thread without sacrificing output and quality from the papermaking machine. This windowed thread, known as "Stardust", was first used in the £20 note issued in 1970. Stardust has been a very great success and is now also used in the £10 and £50 notes, as well as having been sold to other countries including Malaysia, Turkey and Sri Lanka.

Threads have been used in banknotes for almost fifty years and so have stood the test of time as an invaluable security device. With the further enhancements that are planned, they will be a very useful feature for many years to come.

Detail from the Series D £10 note showing windowed thread security device

The web printing process

After the Second World War, a Research Section was set up at the Bank of England Printing Works to study and develop banknote production techniques. In 1953 Peter Price was appointed Research Manager to head this Section. Together with Axel Rosswall of the Bank of Sweden, he began to plan the introduction of banknote printing by the web process, with the aim of converting reels of paper into fully printed, machine-examined and sorted banknotes overwrapped in packets of 100, in a single process. But first a whole range of complex technical problems had to be solved, not least that of automated note examination.

First, a research press was built. Starting with a Goebel intaglio unit, the team added in turn a Victory Kidder offset printing unit and numerator, and a note-sorting and -packing unit made by the Thrissell Engineering Company of Bristol; it was truly a composite press. By 1960 this combination had proved effective and a small quantity of the new series of £1 notes was printed on it and issued. Meanwhile an experimental automatic note-examination system was under development with the assistance of Crosfield Electronics Ltd; it was based on the electronic scanning and comparison of two notes placed side by side.

Following the successful test run on the research machine, tenders were invited from several companies for the building of a web press to be used as a production prototype. This was to be based on experience already gained

Web printing at the Bank of England Printing Works

and to incorporate the manufacturing techniques of a single supplier. Two contracts were awarded, one to Goebel for a three-wide web press with sheet delivery and the second to Thrissell for a two-wide web press with an integral note-sorting and -packing unit. The latter assumed that the development of the automated scanning system would reach fruition. The Goebel machine was delivered in 1962 and the Thrissell machine a year or so later.

The electronic comparison scanner concept proved to be ahead of its time, however; the electronics of the day were too unsophisticated to deal with homogeneity of banknote printing, particularly intaglio printing. In 1967, therefore, it was decided to defer the development of an automated examination system until more advanced electronic techniques became available, but to capitalise on the benefits already apparent in the web printing process.

Accordingly four "production" web presses with sheet delivery were ordered from Masson Scott Thrissell (the company of which the Thrissell Engineering Company was now a part) and delivered in 1968 and 1969. Two further web presses of similar design were delivered in 1974. These presses have been in continuous operation since, and together have printed some 20,000 million banknotes.

Aerial view of The Bank of England Printing Works, Loughton, Essex

Computer-aided design

In 1985 a computer-aided design (CAD) system was installed at the Bank of England Printing Works. This was the culmination of many years of development work aimed at producing an electronic design capability that not only could produce more quickly the type of work traditionally associated with geometric lathes (and evident on the current series of English banknotes) but which would also be able to generate and manipulate new varieties of patterns in ways hitherto impossible to achieve.

The system comprises a powerful computer with various peripheral devices driven by a unique software package specially developed for the Bank by the U.K. Atomic Energy Authority. It permits the generation or reproduction of every conceivable type of pattern or image, from linear, geometric or mathematically based patterns (using the keyboard to direct the laser) through freehand, artist produced drawings (using a digitiser) to complex tonal images such as portraits (using a scanner).

Once the necessary information has been input into the computer in either vector or digital form, it can be stored in the memory to be manipulated, repeated, masked or moved around at will, in relation to other design elements. The results are drawn on the high-resolution display screen, and the finalised version can be output direct onto diazo film ready for platemaking. The system therefore constitutes a complete design capability, which can be used at every stage from origination through to the production of masters ready for platemaking.

Note design using the CAD method

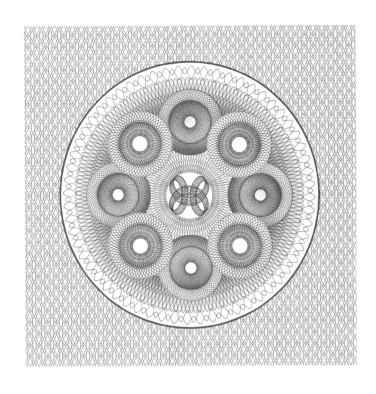

AUSTRIA

The first computerised guilloche machine

A Computer Guilloche Machine (CGM) was installed at the Austrian National Bank's Printing Works in 1982, superseding the guilloche machines previously used. These new machines are used to improve the intricate line patterns or guilloches on banknotes, which not only make the notes very attractive, but are also difficult to counterfeit. The CGM was used in the design of the latest series of banknotes, the issue of which began in 1983.

Line pattern produced by the CAD/CAM system on the CGM

UNITED STATES — COPE equipment

In the final step in U.S. currency printing, the face of the note is overprinted by the letterpress process with several features: the Treasury Seal, the appropriate Federal Reserve District seal with its district letter, the matching district number on each of the four corners of the note and a serial number on each of the halves. The Treasury Seal on Federal Reserve notes and both serial numbers are printed in green, and the Federal Reserve seal and district numbers are printed in black.

The sheets are overprinted and cut into single notes on line, using specialised Currency and Overprinting Processing Equipment (COPE). This prints the serial numbers and seals on the pre-printed currency sheets, collects them into units of 100 sheets and conveys them to cutting knives, which cut the sheets first into two-note units and then into individual notes. Each stack of 100 notes is then banded, and 40 such stacks are packaged into a "brick". Each brick thus contains 4,000 notes, and weighs roughly 4 kg.

Treasury Seal

Serial numbers

Federal Reserve seal

43

CHINA

The dry offset/Orloff multi colour process

The dry offset/Orloff multicolour banknote printing press was invented by Mr Li Genxu, a senior banknote-printing engineer, after research that lasted from 1954 to 1957. It came into use for printing Chinese banknotes (Ren Min Bi) in 1960.

In the printing of background patterns on banknotes, perfectly accurate registration of the lines in the patterns of different colours is necessary as protection against counterfeiting, but is difficult to achieve using traditional offset methods. The dry offset/Orloff multicolour printing press, however, can print in four colours with accurate registration in a single pass. The Orloff machine's structure is novel, incorporating pattern cylinders, distributing cylinders and collecting cylinders; it produces notes that are exquisite works of art and extremely difficult to counterfeit.

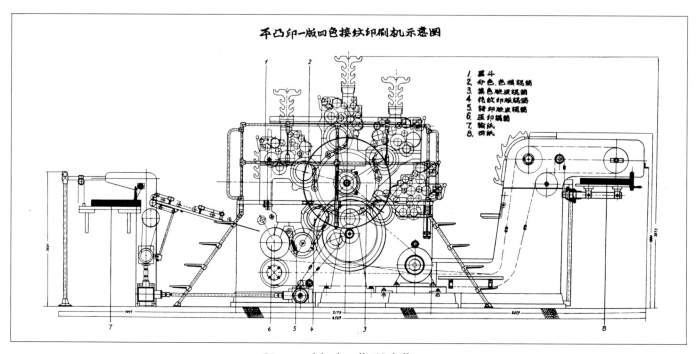

Diagram of the dry offset/Orloff press

Background motifs used on the 1960 two-yuan note

AUSTRALIA

Line-drawing techniques

A significant security feature of Australia's banknotes, which is also used on bonds and travellers' cheques, is the intaglio print (raised printing that can be felt with the fingers). Traditionally the master steel die from which the printing plate is made has been prepared by hand engraving. In Australia, however, a line drawing of the motif – a portrait, for instance – is first made; this drawing exactly corresponds to the image on the finished note. When the artist is satisfied, the image is transferred directly to the master die from which the plate is produced.

Line-drawing technique

This procedure was first used in the 1953 note series, and was further developed for the production of the 1966 decimal series of notes.

Ever since the first Commonwealth note issue of 1913, Australian banknotes have carried distinctive background designs. A Chapman geometric lathe was generally used for this work until the early 1960s, but for the decimal currency series a medallion ruling machine was also used, while in 1972 a Kämpf geometric lathe was added to the design equipment to increase the Bank's capacity to create highly detailed patterns for both intaglio designs and background tints.

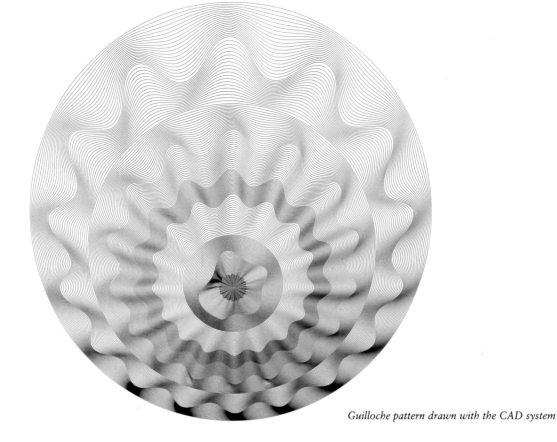

Guilloche pattern drawn with the CAD system

Computer-aided design (CAD) was introduced in 1986. The development of background tint designs was once both lengthy and laborious; however, new computer technology has speeded it up enormously. The artist using computer designing equipment can create designs and alter them, erase and replace details, elongate and distort his patterns at will, all virtually instantaneously. Not only can unique patterns be generated, with consequent improved security; the saving of the designer's time can be dramatic. The guilloche illustrated, for example, was produced in fifteen minutes on the CAD system. A similar design would take at least five days to produce with the geometric lathe.

Printing technology

The first distinctively Australian notes were produced on two Hoe (calico wiping) flatbed machines purchased from Bradbury Wilkinson in 1912, with Dawson, Payne and Elliott Stop Cylinder flatbed letterpress machines (acquired from the Commonwealth Treasury) providing the background tints. Several Hoe (calico wiping) rotary steel plate presses were introduced in 1928, and gradually replaced the two original Hoe units; as the country's currency needs increased, their number rose to thirteen.

Australia's note designs had developed around a combination of Miehle letterpress machines, for the backgrounds, replacing the outdated Stop Cylinder models in the mid-1940s, and Hoe intaglio presses. By the early 1960s they consisted of a two colour letterpress background on one side of the note only, with single-colour intaglio prints on both sides.

Hoe flatbed machine in operation (1913)

Hoe rotary intaglio press (1928)

In 1964, with the forthcoming decimal currency issue in mind, and following worldwide trends in security printing, the bank acquired two Giori Standard Simultan machines, which could print the background colours on both sides of the note simultaneously. This allowed the designers to introduce multicolour backgrounds on both sides of the new notes, and also to incorporate rainbowing (different colours blending into each other). This background treatment was complemented by a single-colour intaglio print on each side of the note, produced by the Hoe rotary presses.

In 1972 the bank purchased two Giori water-wiping intaglio six-colour presses, mainly so that it could increase its production of $1 notes – the intaglio presses print only one side of the note at each pass. The multicolour intaglio capacity of the new presses also meant that their colour capability could be used in intaglio designs; this was exploited in the 1973 $50 note, both sides of which carried multicolour backgrounds complemented by three-colour intaglio prints.

The transfer in 1981 of the Reserve Bank of Australia's note-printing operations to a new plant in Craigieburn, near Melbourne, coincided with the purchase of Giori Super Simultan II and Giori Super Intagliocolour equipment (the

Detail of the Australian $50 note

Super machines are able to handle larger sheets at faster running speeds than can the older presses). New Supernumerota numbering machinery was also acquired to supplement the existing installation and to take over the work being handled by the older Heidelberg numbering units. The design of the $100 note in 1984 drew upon the additional background colour capacity of the Giori Super Simultan: it used eight plates – four on each side of the note – all with rainbowing.

A further useful advance was the development of fast-setting intaglio inks in the early 1980s; this made it possible to abandon the time-consuming practice of putting interleaves between the sheets after intaglio printing (and of course later disinterleaving them).

The plastic banknote

Following a well-organised attempt in 1966 to counterfeit the new $10 note, the Reserve Bank of Australia had to consider whether adequate security could be attained using current technology. Any new note needed to fulfil three basic requirements: it had to be easily identifiable as genuine by the holder, it had to be difficult to counterfeit or simulate successfully, and it had to be durable and robust enough to withstand normal handling.

In 1968 the Commonwealth Scientific and Industrial Research Organisation (CSIRO) was asked to undertake research into alternative substrate materials and security features. After preliminary studies of new types of paper using natural fibres, the focus shifted to a substrate based on a polymer (plastic). The main security feature proposed for the new note became known as an Optically Variable Device (OVD) and was based on well-known optical principles.

After extensive research, the Bank and CSIRO launched the Currency Notes Research and Development Project. During this development phase, the experimental notes were tested to the limit: they were folded, torn, rubbed, stained with anything from gravy to engine oil to beer, exposed to every kind of weather, buried in soil and even laundered in a domestic washing machine.

Once the experimental polymer-based notes had been proved to be satisfactory in use, mass-production techniques were developed. The approach of Australia's bicentennial year of 1988 led the Bank to decide to introduce the new technology in the form of a commemorative $10 note, to be issued only in that year. The note, which is the same size as the existing note (155 mm × 77.5 mm) was released on 27 January 1988. The issue of the standard note has continued.

The commemorative note has several security features that are not carried by other Australian notes. The OVD, a portrait of Captain Cook, is visible from either side of the note; it diffracts light, producing a varying rainbow pattern when the viewing angle or the angle of the light source is changed. It has a transparent surround; itself a

Commemorative $10 note issued 1988, detail of OVD on "supply side"

Bicentennial commemorative note of 1988, front and back

simple but important security device. An area of wave patterns is produced early in the manufacturing process; although it is covered with offset printing, the pattern can be seen in some parts of the design when the note is held up to the light. Complementary diamond-shaped patterns are printed on both sides of the note, and these register perfectly when the note is viewed against the light. Microlettering (just above the ship's deck) also provides security, while the two serial numbers on each note are printed in different typefaces and colours.

Harry Williamson, the designer of Australia's $100 note, was chosen to design the new note, aided by the staff at the Bank's Note Printing Branch. The theme of the design is settlement. One side of the note shows the ship *Supply* of the First Fleet, together with a medley of people against a background of Sydney Cove. The other side relates to Australia's first inhabitants. It brings together some elements of Aboriginal culture – ancient rock painting and hand stencils, an Aboriginal youth wearing body paint and a Morning Star Pole; the pole is the work of the Aboriginal artist Yumbulul and is the kind of pole used by the Aboriginal people of north-east Arnhem Land on certain ceremonial occasions. Some designs by Aboriginal artists have been used to inspire background patterns.

*Design elements for the $10 note, 1988, showing motifs of the
Aboriginal culture and the history of settlement since 1788*

COUNTERFEITERS INTERNATIONAL

Throughout history, and in every country of the world, it has always been regarded as a crime to counterfeit legal tender, and convicted counterfeiters were liable to the death penalty until well into the nineteenth century.

For example, Chinese currency notes of the early Ming dynasty (1368–1644) carried the warning: "Whosoever forges notes or circulates counterfeit notes shall be beheaded. Whosoever reports and apprehends a counterfeiter shall receive a reward of 250 silver tael and the counterfeiter's entire property."

Similar warnings, though less drastically phrased, were displayed on some central banks' notes; Austrian banknotes, for example, warned: "Counterfeiting or forging the notes of the Bank carries the same punishment as counterfeiting or forging the paper currency issued by the State. It is the duty of the authorities to find, apprehend and punish such criminals."

Warning on the 100-Deutsche mark banknote dated 2 January 1960

AUSTRIA

The first warning on Austrian banknotes appeared on the 1841 series. These notes were designed by the renowned Biedermeier painter Peter Fendi and were remarkably beautiful; moreover, they were intaglio-printed and were believed counterfeit-proof at that time. Chief Accountant Salzmann even defended the enormous cost of adapting the Printing Works for the new process against official objection by arguing that no more counterfeit notes would appear in the future.

The warning was intented to deter counterfeiters, but no one knows whether this, or any other written admonition, ever had such an effect. It certainly did not stop one Austrian master-forger, Peter Ritter von Bohr – indeed, the printing quality of the warning on his counterfeit notes was unusually good!

*Water-colour painting
by the Biedermeier artist Peter Fendi*

53

The case of the master-counterfeiter

Peter Ritter von Bohr was born in 1772, and as a young man was immensely rich; by the time he was forty, he was supposed to have amassed a fortune of 130,000 Gulden on the stock exchange. When the "Banco Zettel" were devalued as a result of Emperor Franz I of Austria's "bankruptcy patent" and many of the rich lost their fortunes, Bohr's huge wealth seemed all the more impressive. He moved from Linz, then a sleepy provincial town, to the Austrian imperial capital Vienna, buying property nearby in Mauer and Erlaa, and Kottingbrunn Castle. He managed to gain access to high society and in 1836 was mentioned in *Oesterreichs Ehrenspiegel*, the *Who's Who* of the day.

After a while, however, Bohr's business ventures began to fare badly. In 1839 he filed a declaration of bankruptcy in Vienna – a very difficult step to take for a man with his background. By 1844, though, Bohr had regained his fortune – by his own endeavours and with the help of his wife Mathilde.

On 23 August 1845, expertly forged 10- and 100-Gulden notes of the "Privilegirte Oesterreichische National-Bank", dated 1 January 1841, were discovered in circulation.

The police officer in charge of the investigation, Commissioner Köpp von Felsenthal, produced a list of people who had the skills necessary for producing these high-quality counterfeits. Bohr's name was on the list; he was already known to the police, because five years earlier he had been accused of passing a forged bill. When Mathilde Bohr was found to have used counterfeit money to pay for a somewhat unusual watch, Köpp acted: he went to the Bohrs' house in Meidling, near Vienna, at seven in the morning on 8 October 1845, with a search warrant and several other officers. In his report he described what he found:

> "What became immediately clear upon searching Bohr's bedroom and den and supported the conviction that Bohr – in spite of the weak eyesight of which he was always complaining – must have worked on copperplate engraving, electrotyping and drawings until very recently, was the amount of gravers, engraving needles, the twenty-two different magnifying glasses and the many copper and zinc plates found. . . .

> "However, Bohr declared that these tools were the remnants of his former artistic activity. Since his left eye had gone completely blind and the sight of his right eye had severely diminished following his cataract operation, he had not exercised this activity for a long time. . . ."

Nothing more was found, but Bohr was arrested and remanded in custody; he was interrogated for days on end, but did not confess. Mathilde Bohr was then arrested – and confessed. On the basis of her evidence, the police went back to the house. This time they were successful: they found a large quantity of forged ten-Gulden notes hidden in an old lathe. This was enough to prove Bohr's guilt. After an unsuccessful suicide bid, the old man admitted to having counterfeited notes and securities for many years, although he maintained that he had only produced as much as he personally needed at a time, and in gentlemanly fashion he denied that his wife knew about his activities. Moreover, after his confession and during his subsequent detention he voluntarily produced engravings and proof prints to prove his special talents – perhaps the only forger ever to help the police in this way. At the time, the Austrian censorship prohibited any reports on the trial, so not a word about the Bohrs reached the newspapers.

Counterfeiter produced by Peter Ritter von Bohr

On 23 March 1846, a panel of judges pronounced the pair guilty and Peter and Mathilde were both sentenced to death by hanging. Later, Emperor Ferdinand I "the Kind" commuted the death sentence into ten years imprisonment for Bohr and two years for his wife.

Mathilde Bohr, who suffered from some severe nervous disorder, was released after just a year in prison; Peter von Bohr died during the second year of his imprisonment.

ENGLAND

The prevention of counterfeiting and forgery of banknotes has always been a subject of concern to the Bank of England. Only three years after its founding in 1694, an Act of Parliament laid down that the forgery or alteration of a banknote was a "felony without the benefit of clergy". This curious expression meant that although anyone found guilty of forgery could be sentenced to death, those in holy orders were exempt – and in those days one could claim that exemption simply by proving that one could read and write. Despite the savagery of the punishment, forgery and counterfeiting continued and many people were hanged. One prisoner saved himself in 1722 by co-operating with the Bank who sent a clerk to interview him for information on ways to combat forgery. As a result the prisoner's death sentence was commuted to transportation for life. A public outcry, excited partly by Cruikshank's "Bank Restriction Note" cartoon, brought about the abolition of the death sentence for counterfeiting in 1832.

George Cruikshank's "Bank Restriction Note" of 1818 –
a protest against the number of executions for forgery
during the Bank Restriction period

Today the equipment used to counterfeit currency has changed, but the risks remain high. For example, following the uttering of some counterfeit £20 notes in south London in 1982, the police stopped a gold Rolls Royce travelling down the Old Kent Road. In the back they found counterfeits with a face value of £500,000. Rather more – about £5 million worth – together with some printing plates were later recovered from a somewhat humbler white Ford Transit van. From the evidence, the police were able to discover that the notes had been produced at a back-street print-shop in London's East End; in order to avoid suspicion, the forgers kept all the "evidence" in the white van during normal working hours. Following the trial at the Old Bailey, the ringleader was sentenced to eight years in prison whilst other members of the gang were sent down for anything from eighteen months to five years.

One of the 7,000 varieties of legal notes circulating during the US Civil War

The birth of the Secret Service

The U.S. Civil War of 1861–65 was the all-time heyday of American forgers: perhaps as much as a third of the paper money in circulation at the time was spurious. The currency system of the day gave the counterfeiters an unparallelled opportunity. Every one of about 1,600 state and private banks issued its own currency and designed its own notes; with around 7,000 varieties of legal notes in circulation, people could hardly be expected to recognise 4,000 types of bogus currency.

It was expected that counterfeiting would end when a national currency was introduced in 1863. The hope proved vain, and the flood of fraudulent notes pouring into circulation made new deterrents an urgent necessity. The U.S. Secret Service was founded on 5 July 1865, and given as one of its primary tasks the elimination of dollar forgery. Although the Secret Service has minimised counterfeiting, this crime continues to threaten the American economy, and today it is on the increase once again. The following Secret Service report was released in 1985.

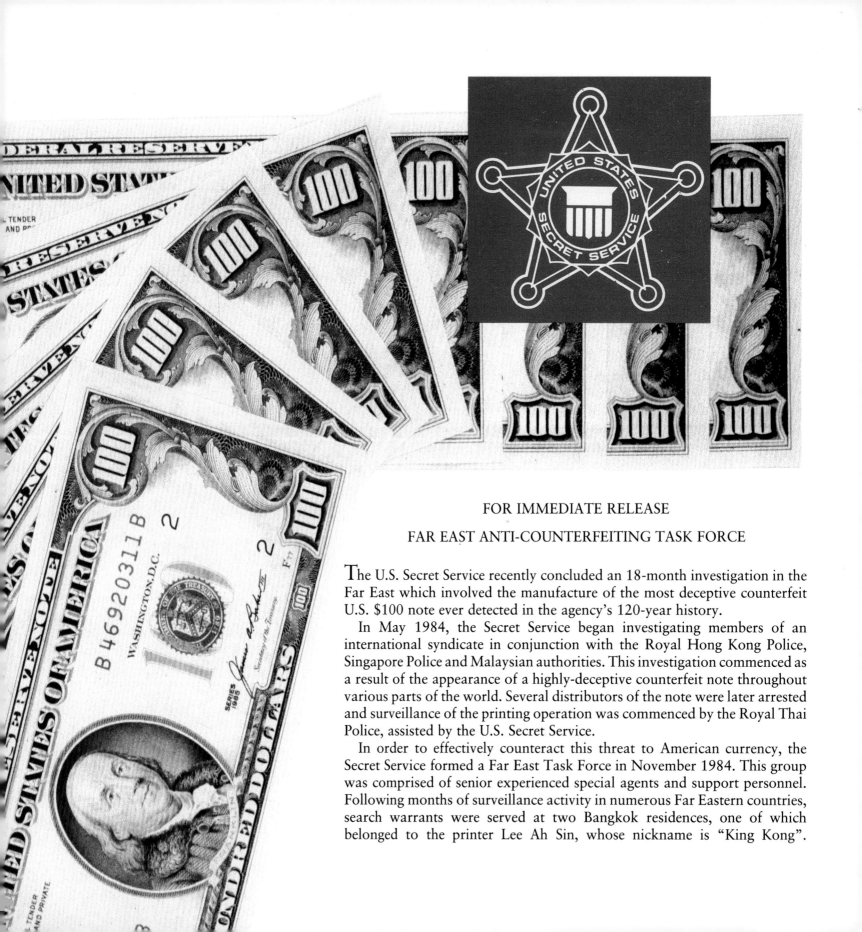

FOR IMMEDIATE RELEASE

FAR EAST ANTI-COUNTERFEITING TASK FORCE

The U.S. Secret Service recently concluded an 18-month investigation in the Far East which involved the manufacture of the most deceptive counterfeit U.S. $100 note ever detected in the agency's 120-year history.

In May 1984, the Secret Service began investigating members of an international syndicate in conjunction with the Royal Hong Kong Police, Singapore Police and Malaysian authorities. This investigation commenced as a result of the appearance of a highly-deceptive counterfeit note throughout various parts of the world. Several distributors of the note were later arrested and surveillance of the printing operation was commenced by the Royal Thai Police, assisted by the U.S. Secret Service.

In order to effectively counteract this threat to American currency, the Secret Service formed a Far East Task Force in November 1984. This group was comprised of senior experienced special agents and support personnel. Following months of surveillance activity in numerous Far Eastern countries, search warrants were served at two Bangkok residences, one of which belonged to the printer Lee Ah Sin, whose nickname is "King Kong".

Equipment and materials used to produce the counterfeit U.S. $100 note were seized by the Royal Thai Police. Additionally, an engraved plate to be used for producing a new counterfeit U.S. $50 note was recovered. Evidence was later discovered that implicated Lee Ah Sin as the printer of counterfeit Malaysian and United Arab Emirates currencies, as well as Visa travellers cheques.

Lee Ah Sin claimed to have developed his counterfeiting skills under the tutelage of Wong Tim Cheung, a master-counterfeiter from Hong Kong, who had been previously arrested for counterfeiting activities. Wong died several years ago. Using processes similar to those employed by the U.S. Bureau of Engraving and Printing, Lee Ah Sin made improvements on Wong's counterfeit negatives and produced, by his own admission, over 2½ million dollars in counterfeit currency.

Laws and court rulings

Section 8 of title 18 of the United States Code states, "the term, obligation or other security of the United States includes all bonds, certificates of indebtedness, national bank currency, Federal Reserve notes, Federal Reserve bank notes, coupons, United States notes, Treasury notes, gold certificates, silver certificates, fractional notes, certificates of deposit, bills, cheques, or drafts for money, drawn by or upon authorised officers of the United States, stamps and other representatives of value, of whatever denomination, issued under any Act of Congress, and cancelled United States stamps."

Section 474 of title 18 of the United States Code states, in relevant part, that "whoever" has in his possession or custody . . . any obligation or other security made or executed, in whole or in part, after the similitude of any obligation issued under the authority of the United States . . . or . . . prints, photographs, or in any other manner makes or executes any engraving, photograph, print, or impression in the likeness of any such obligation or other security, or any part thereof . . . shall be fined not more than $5,000 or imprisoned not more than fifteen years or both."

Section 475 of title 18 of the United States Code further restricts the manufacture and use of illustrations of obligations and securities of the United States and provides, in relevant part, that "whoever designs, engraves, prints, makes, or executes, or utters, issues, distributes, circulates, or uses any business or professional card, notice placard, circular, handbill, or advertisement in the likeness or similitude of any obligation or security of the United States . . . shall be fined not more than $500."

Section 504 of title 18 of the United States Code, however, makes an exception to these prohibitions and permits the reproduction of obligations and securities of the United States provided such illustrations are in black and white and are of a size less than three-quarters or more than one and one-half, in linear dimension, of each part of the item illustrated.

In *Regan v Time, Inc.*, the United States Supreme Court held that "the color and size limitations (of 18 U.S.C. 504) are . . . reasonable manner regulations that can constitutionally be imposed on those wishing to publish photographic reproductions of currency." In view of the Supreme Court's ruling, it is the position of the Department of Treasury, in which the Department of Justice concurs, that illustrations of currency and other obligations and securities of the United States may be used for any non-fraudulent purpose, including advertising, provided that the illustration conforms to the size and colour limitations specified in section 504.

AUSTRALIA

Coat of Arms

At the time of Federation – 1 January 1901 – the newly formed Australian Commonwealth Government assumed the right to print the new nation's banknotes. The authority was not exercised until the Australian Notes Act came into force in 1910, however, and it was another three years before the first truly Australian banknote (the Commonwealth of Australia ten-shilling note) was issued.

Under the provisions of the Reserve Bank Act 1959, the Reserve Bank of Australia now has the exclusive authority to print, issue, re-issue and cancel Australian notes.

A forged ten-shilling note bearing the serial number M536739 appeared on 30 December 1914; this was the first known forgery of the new Australian banknote. There have been a number of subsequent attempts, for since then every Australian note issue has been counterfeited to some extent and, as with the 1914 ten-shilling note, usually within two years of its issue. In spite of the forgers' persistence, however, only one of their notes (the 1966 $10 counterfeit) reached the public in any significant numbers. Those responsible for the rest were caught either before distribution of the counterfeit had begun, or when only a few notes had been passed.

Up to 1974, Australian counterfeiters largely confined themselves to Australian currency, but since then the counterfeiting of foreign currencies, especially U.S. currency, has been on the increase: one incident involved counterfeits of more than U.S. $15 million in value.

Several owners of small printing businesses have tried to solve their cash flow problems by counterfeiting. The poor standard of nearly all their notes may indicate why their businesses were in difficulties! The counterfeit, illustrated, for instance, has an obvious error in the line "throughout Australia and its Territories" in which the "and" appears as an ampersand "&".

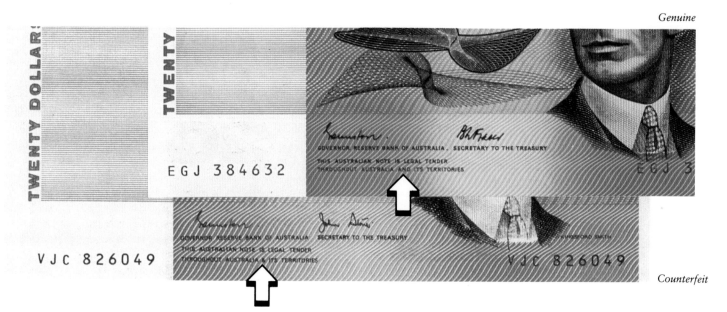

Genuine

Counterfeit

CHINA

Genuine

Counterfeit

China's most serious banknote counterfeiting case was uncovered on 6 May 1982, when more than 61,000 counterfeit ten-yuan Ren Min Bi (RMB) notes, smuggled in from Hong Kong, were seized in Shenzhen City, Guangdong Province, and 1,200 similar notes were found in eighteen other counties and cities, including Guangzhou, Shantou, and some of the counties of Fujiang Province, such as Nanping. Six days later, 11,928 identical notes were discovered on the coast of Hong Kong. Such large numbers and such a wide distribution of counterfeits had never been recorded in China before.

On the evening of the same day, the Royal Hong Kong Police shut down the counterfeit workshop at On Wah Industrial Building, Fotan Village, Shatin, Hong Kong, and arrested the counterfeiters. At the workshop 37,560 partially printed ten-yuan counterfeit notes were awaiting completion, for which the necessary equipment was all ready: a Japanese-made "Hamada" automatic mono-colour press, four PS plates, a printing-down frame, a guillotine, ink and photochemicals. The finished and unfinished counterfeit notes discovered had a total face value of RMB 1,116,880 yuan.

The counterfeiters had used a colour photocopier, an offset printing press and ordinary offset paper to simulate a Chinese intaglio-printed ten-yuan RMB note. The counterfeit notes could easily be detected by eye and by feel. The watermark on the genuine note had been imitated by printing with greyish-white ink, so no watermark shade could be seen on the reverse of the printed image, and the characteristic intaglio texture of course was missing.

GOVERNMENTS AS COUNTERFEITERS

Governments have been prepared to use forged banknotes to ruin an enemy's economy for at least two hundred years. The British were pioneers in the field: during the American War of Independence (1775–83), under the orders of King George III, they uttered a huge number of false Continental bills (see page 296). Together with the inflation of the circulation through the Continental Congress, these British forgeries were principally responsible for the later devaluation of the Continental bills.

Counterfeiting: the secret weapon

The paper money (Banco-Zettel) issued by the Wiener-Stadt-Banco from 1762 included every safeguard against forgery known to makers. Napoleon Bonaparte, self-proclaimed Emperor of France since 1804, was as unimpressed by the security features as he was by the death penalty warning. During the occupation of Vienna in 1806, he ordered his troops under General Clark to copy the Banco-Zettel printing plates and to confiscate the originals, and then had extremely good Banco-Zettel counterfeits printed in Paris and Italy.

Napoleon Bonaparte's signature

A Napoleonic fake

Napoleon also ordered the counterfeiting of Russian banknotes, and is said to have considered the forging of English currency as well, but never had the chance to put that plan into practice.

England came under suspicion in its turn after World War I, in which Austria-Hungary fought as one of the Central Powers along with the German Reich, Bulgaria and Turkey. In the last few months of the war Austrian officials came to believe they had evidence that England was planning to smuggle counterfeit Austrian banknotes into the country. On 21 August 1918, the following confidential letter was sent to the branches and business departments of the Austro-Hungarian Bank:

> "A trustworthy source has disclosed that the notes of the Austro-Hungarian Bank are to be counterfeited in England for smuggling into the country so as to jeopardise the Monarch's economic interests. Thus the suspicion that the Entente will use all means, especially exchange transports of invalids coming from England, to smuggle the false notes, is well founded . . ."

Austria-Hungary's defeat in World War I was followed by the dissolution of the "Danube Monarchy" in the autumn of

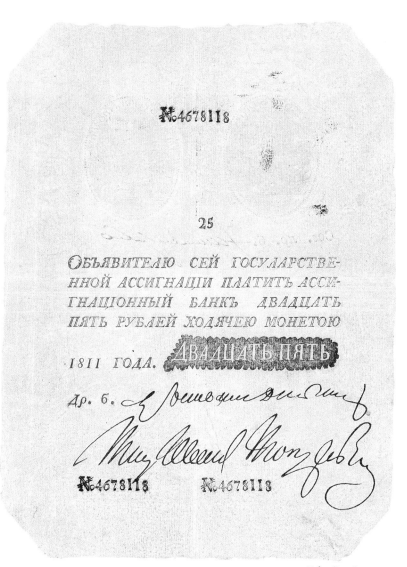

False Russian note, counterfeited on Napoleon's orders

25-Kronen note, produced in private print shops

1918. The successor states (Czechoslovakia and Hungary) then issued unauthorised notes of their own. Those produced under Bela Kun's Hungarian Communist government are especially interesting. During the regime's brief five months of power in 1919, immense numbers of forged Austro-Hungarian banknotes in denominations of one, two, 25 and 200 Kronen were produced in private print-shops from the original plates. The one- and two-Kronen counterfeits were later exchanged by the Hungarian government at their full face value; the 25- and 200-Kronen notes were redeemed at only one-fifth of their nominal value.

"Operation Bernhard"

Forged notes recovered from Lake Toplitz

During the nineteenth and early twentieth centuries, all the Bank of England's notes looked very much alike, differing only in the wording and the signatures. They were difficult to forge, however, mainly because of their intricately patterned watermark. One counterfeiter was not deterred, however: Adolf Hitler, Führer and Chancellor of the Third Reich.

During World War II, Hitler ordered the production of perfect imitations of British banknote paper complete with watermark, in a top-secret operation. The SS installed a fully equipped printing works in the Oranienburg concentration camp near Berlin, and prisoners there worked with highly qualified printers to produce very high-quality faked British pound notes; the counterfeiting of U.S. dollar bills was also planned.

The project, christened "Operation Bernhard", served the Third Reich well. The Reich's intelligence service used the false notes to buy weapons and foreign currency abroad and, it is said, to pay the famous spy "Cicero" and Mussolini's liberator Skorzeny as well. As the end of the war approached, the fakes were dumped at the bottom of Lake Toplitz, near Salzburg. Divers have since recovered the "treasure". The coming of peace prevented further, and perhaps worse, catastrophes.

COUNTERFEITS CLASSIFIED

Most forgers use one of three methods: printing counterfeit notes, altering genuine notes, or drawing counterfeit notes by hand. We shall look in detail at three forged German notes, which between them illustrate the three methods.

Printed counterfeit notes

Counterfeit note

Genuine note

The genuine Braunschweigische Bank ten-thaler courant note shown, dated 1 May 1854 measures 158 × 88 mm; the counterfeit is just a millimetre wider. The paper of the counterfeit is lighter in colour than that of the genuine note; it has no watermark. The note recognised as a counterfeit was marked by hand with the words "This banknote is counterfeit" and confirmed by two signatures.

The genuine note features the words "BRAUNSCHW. BANKNOTE" in the lower, unprinted part bordered by a frame and "10 THLR 10" on both sides, also in a frame.

Altered notes

By far the most common type of alteration is a change in the note's value; the Penal Code defines "alteration" as changing a genuine note to give the impression that its value is higher. The note shown here is a real 100-Reichsmark Reichsbank banknote dated 11 October 1924, on which zeros have been added to make the value 100 appear as 1,000. The counterfeit note measures 180 × 90 mm, whereas a genuine 1,000-Reichsmark Reichsbank banknote measures 190 × 95 mm. The alteration to the lettering is easily seen.

*Front of the genuine
100-Reichsmark Reichsbank banknote*

*Alteration of the
100-Reichsmark Reichsbank banknote(back)*

*Back of the genuine
1,000-Reichsmark Reichsbank banknote*

*Back of the
genuine banknote*

Alteration of the 100-Reichsmark Reichsbank banknote (front)

Front of the genuine 1,000-Reichsmark Reichsbank banknote

Hand-drawn notes

Generally only a few notes are made in this way and they show paper defects: optical security features such as the watermark and the security thread are usually missing. Details of the drawing are usually fuzzy and coarse compared to the original, or have a slightly different colour. The spacing of the letters and numerals is irregular, and these are not always in a straight line.

These features can be seen in this counterfeit Bank deutscher Länder 50-Deutsche mark banknote of the 1948 series. It is the same width as the genuine note, but a millimetre less in height.

Hand-drawn forgery (front)

The genuine banknote

68

INTERPOL AND THE COUNTERFEITER

Interpol – the International Criminal Police Organisation – was founded at the Vienna International Police Congress of 1923 on the initiative of the Vienna Chief of Police Johann Schober. The organisation was set up to deal with crimes that cross national frontiers, such as drug-trafficking, smuggling, and note and coin counterfeiting.

During the conference, governments of all countries were asked to set up central offices to deal with counterfeiting. These central offices were to co-operate via an international office, initially in Vienna. The task of Interpol headquarters (Paris-based since 1946) is to "take note of all incidents related to counterfeiting or the alteration of money and public registered bonds; to record all cases of such forgery brought to its attention as well as the names of the counterfeiters and their accomplices; to inform the authorities responsible for dealing with suspected counterfeiters and the Central offices abroad about noteworthy perceptions and news on such issues; to arrange for the exchange of identification aids photographs, fingerprint registers of counterfeiters and their accomplices and to file and store the counterfeits or copies thereof" (excerpt from a circular to all members of the newly founded Interpol in 1923).

1924 saw the first appearance of *Contrefaçons et Falsifications*, a publication intended to help police authorities and financial institutions to act against currency and security document counterfeiting. This publication contained reports on forgeries, new issues and withdrawals from circulation; the reports still appear today, in loose-leaf form.

Warrants of arrest from the Interpol publication "Contrefaçons et Falsifications"

HOW TO FRUSTRATE COUNTERFEITERS AND FORGERS

No one knows how to stop counterfeiters trying to produce and utter faked banknotes. Nevertheless banknote printers can make life extremely risky for forgers, by using manufacturing techniques that are difficult to imitate and by teaching people how to distinguish genuine notes from counterfeits.

The techniques of note manufacture are steadily being improved, and electronically controlled printing presses now allow unprecedented precision in production. But this counterfeit deterrence is ineffective until as many members of the public as possible are familiar with the security features of the banknotes they use, and can recognise them.

People all over the world pass money without a second glance, and counterfeiters happily exploit their carelessness. Often they do not even try to produce perfect facsimiles; a cheap reproduction, just good enough to fool a casual observer, is enough to give them a profit. If, however, users could instantly recognise funny money, the distributors of false notes would run a very real risk of being caught – and to catch a distributor quickly, perhaps because a waiter, a petrol court attendant or a taxidriver realises that the note is false, improves the police's chance of pinpointing the production source of the counterfeits enormously. In such a case they are close to the first distributor; once counterfeit currency has been passed unrecognised by five, ten or twenty users, it becomes much harder to trace it back and to shut down the production facilities.

Interpol's worldwide network therefore sees consumer education as a useful way of improving its chances of success against the counterfeiters. This is why many countries, as well as producing currency of excellent technical quality are now turning their attention to informing the public thoroughly about its most important security features.

SPAIN:
information brochures

When the most recent series of Spanish notes was issued, full information about their security features was provided in brochures produced for each denomination. They included information in English, French and Spanish about the security features that can be recognised by the naked eye, in ultra-violet light or by using electronic detectors.

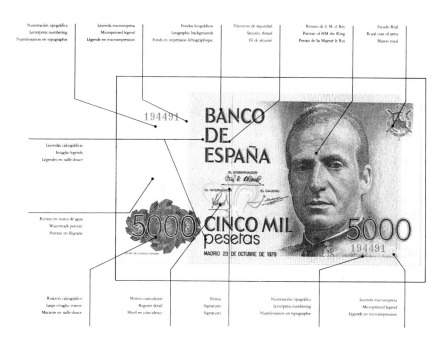

Numeración tipográfica
Letterpress numbering
Numération en typographie

Leyenda microimpresa
Microprinted legend
Légende en microimpression

Fondos litográficos
Litographic backgrounds
Fonds en impression lithographique

Filamento de seguridad
Security thread
Fil de sécurité

Retrato de S. M. el Rey
Portrait of HM the King
Portrait de Sa Majesté le Roi

Escudo Real
Royal coat of arms
Blason royal

Leyendas calcográficas
Intaglio legends
Légendes en taille-douce

Retrato en marca de agua
Watermark portrait
Portrait en filigrane

Roseta calcográfica
Large intaglio rosette
Macaron en taille-douce

Motivo coincidente
Register detail
Motif en coincidence

Firmas
Signatures
Signatures

Numeración tipográfica
Letterpress numbering
Numération en typographie

Leyenda microimpresa
Microprinted legend
Légende en microimpression

Description of the 1979 5,000-peseta note (front)

Defensa contra la falsificación
Protection against forgery
Résistance à la contrefaçon

El creciente peligro de las falsificaciones, que afecta ya a la mayor parte de los países, aconseja la conservación y mejora de los elementos tradicionales de seguridad y la incorporación de otros más modernos, con el propósito de dificultar la ejecución de aquéllas y facilitar el reconocimiento de los billetes auténticos.

El nuevo sistema está dotado de los siguientes elementos, que son observables:

a) *A simple vista:*
   – Gran retrato en el anverso y viñeta en el reverso impresos en calcografía multicolor.
   – Marca de agua.
   – Elemento de coincidencia perfecta en anverso y reverso.
   – Filamento de seguridad.

b) *Con luz ultravioleta:*
   – Papel no fluorescente.
   – Fibrillas fluorescentes de color rojo y verde amarillento.
   – Determinados efectos que se especifican para cada billete en particular.

The growing danger of forgeries, which now affect most countries, makes it advisable to retain and improve the traditional security features and incorporate other, more modern ones with the aim of making forgery more difficult and the authentic notes easier to recognise.

The new system has the following features, which are discernible

a) *To the na...*
   – Large po...
     nette on...
     colour ir...
   – Waterm...
   – Detail d...
     between...
   – Security...

b) *Under ul...*
   – Non-flu...
   – Fluoresc...
     fibres.
   – Specific...
     individu...

Le risque de plus en plus grand de contrefaçon qui existe dans la majorité des pays milite en faveur du maintien et de l'amélioration des éléments traditionnels de sécurité, et de l'introduction d'autres éléments plus modernes, afin de rendre plus difficiles ces contrefaçons et de faciliter la reconnaissance des billets authentiques.

La nouvelle série de billets est dotée

Fibres in banknote paper

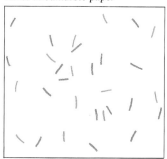

Descriptions of security features in three languages

SWEDEN: information leaflets

The Bank of Sweden has also started a comprehensive information campaign on its banknotes' security features, in which it describes the designs and points out the main features in detail. It has also issued an illustrated description of the banknotes that were no longer legal tender after 31 December 1987.

De nya sedlarna
100 kronor

Sveriges Riksbank

I sedelnumret kan man utläsa vilket år sedeln är tryckt. Den första siffran i numret är densamma som sista siffran i tryck-året. Andra och tredje siffran visar vilket decennium sedeln är tryckt enligt en speciell kod.

Teckningen av polli-nerande växter är hämtad från en plansch ur Linnés ungdomsverk *Præludia Sponsaliarum Plantarum* från 1729.

Bakom växterna ligger en bild av den botaniska trädgård i Uppsala, som Linné förestod, nuvarande Linnéträdgården.

Till höger om Linnés porträtt återges ett av hans valspråk i mikrotext, *Omnia mirari etiam tritissima* (förundra dig över allt, även det mest alldagliga). Ovan-på mikrotexten ligger en faksimil av Linnés handskrift.

1. Vattenmärket framställs redan vid tillverkningen av sedelpappret. Det består av förtunningar och för-tjockningar, som bildar ett mönster. Vattenmärket i 100-kronorssedeln upprepar framsidans porträtt av Linné. Säkerhetstråden syns som en mörk linje när sedeln hålls mot ljuset.

2. Den svarta triangeln i sedelns högra kant innehåller en dold bild (latent image). Det innebär att en mindre triangel graverats inuti den större. Den lilla triangeln syns bara om man håller sedeln vågrätt mot ljuset och lutar den något ifrån sig.

3. Längst upp till höger på sedelns framsida finns en mikrotext inlagd i guillochemönstrets slingor. Det är ett av Linnés mest kända valspråk »Omnia mirari etiam tritissima». Mikrotexten har gjorts osymmetrisk i höjdled och bildar därigenom ett vågformigt mönster.

4. De nya sedlarna trycks med en avancerad tryckteknik. 100-kronors-sedeln är framställd i både offsettryck (plantryck) och koppartryck (djup-tryck). Det graverade mönstret i t.ex. Linnés porträtt ger i koppartryck en reliefverkan som kan kännas med fingret.

Part of an information leaflet issued in 1987

UNITED STATES: *know your money*

The U.S. dollar bill turns up in nearly every country, and is the most commonly forged note in the world; even so, compared to the total circulation of dollar notes, the percentage of forgeries is tiny. *Know your money* is a booklet published by the U.S. Secret Service to inform the public about the most important features of the dollar bill; it is available in several languages.

As well as hints on how to recognise false money, the booklet also gives advice on what to do when you receive what you recognise to be counterfeit or forged currency: do not return it to the passer; delay him if possible; telephone the police; note his description, the description of an accomplice (if there is one) and the licence number of any vehicle used; write your initials and the date on the edge of the note; touch the note as little as possible, so that you do not smudge any fingerprints, and put it into an envelope; surrender the note only to the police.

The American information booklet

Serial numbers

73

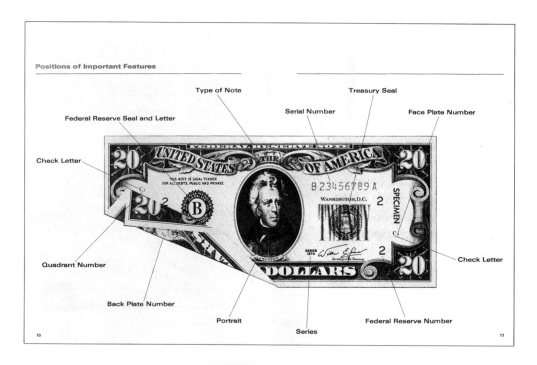

Positions of Important Features

Type of Note

Treasury Seal

Serial Number

Face Plate Number

Federal Reserve Seal and Letter

Check Letter

Quadrant Number

Back Plate Number

Portrait

Series

Check Letter

Federal Reserve Number

Counterfeit-Genuine

Counterfeit-Genuine

Counterfeit-Genuine

AUSTRIA: a co-ordinated approach

There has been no large-scale counterfeiting of banknotes in Austria for some forty years, though a few isolated, primitive fakes have been made by photocopying or collage. There are three main reasons for this: it is expensive to produce large amounts of forged or counterfeit notes which can only be passed in a small country, Austrian banknotes have a large number of deterrent features; and a greater public awareness of the features of the notes has increased the risks taken in passing counterfeit money.

This last deterrent is a direct result of the information campaign, which focuses on the five main features of the banknotes: the texture of the intaglio printing, the tilting effect, the register ornament, the watermark and the security thread. Several co-ordinated measures have contributed to its success, requiring a high degree of co-operation between the Central Bank, the commercial banks and the postal service.

Since 1983 (when the latest series of notes was issued) information and discussion sessions have been held annually for representatives of the major commercial banks and for top officials of Interpol in Austria, who are also shown a small exhibition on the security of Austrian banknotes and on the Schilling hard currency.

Since 1983, press conferences have also been held whenever a new note is launched, to publicise the note's special security features, its appearance and its manufacture.

Banks, post offices and schools have displayed posters outlining the main features of each of the latest series of notes, and have distributed over 5,000,000 information leaflets during the past five years.

Description of 50-Schilling note, 1986, leaflet detail

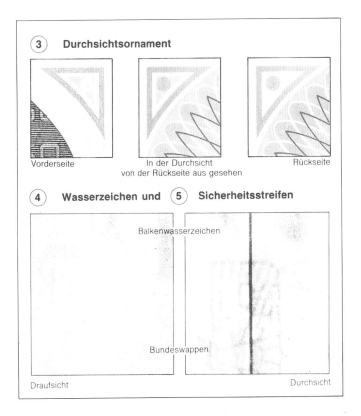

The campaign aimed not only to teach people, but also to encourage them to apply their knowledge. So a draw, with new banknotes worth 1,000 Schillings as prizes, was set up to capture the public's attention. Entry forms and information leaflets were available at all bank and post office counters; people entering the draw entered the five security features on their form and sent it back to the Austrian National Bank. The contest lasted for six months after the issue of each note, and ten winners were drawn every month. Around 100,000 entries were sent in during the first six weeks of the first contest, and by the time that four new notes had been issued more than 750,000 forms had been received. A return of 1,000,000 entries (Austria has a population of 7,000,000) is expected by the end of the campaign.

Austrian schools teach basic facts about banknotes to eight- to ten-year-olds, and then review and enlarge upon the topic to the ten- to fifteen-year-old group. The Austrian National Bank, jointly with the Ministry of Education, Art and Sports, organised a schools programme to supplement this teaching. All 3,900 primary schools were provided

Poster describing the 1986 50-Schilling note   *Information leaflet*

Reply card

Worksheet for Austrian schools

with a package including worksheets, a poster of each new banknote, information leaflets for teachers, overhead projection sheets on banknote security features and the gold backing of the Austrian currency, and an order form for additional worksheets.

The centrepiece of the package was the worksheet which described banknote security features in a way suited to the children's age group, with the five features symbolised by the five digits of the hand. The younger children were challenged to find the security features in a picture of part of a banknote. Older children had to complete statements on their worksheets about the security features, and their replies could be cut out and sent in as entries to a further draw. Twice a year – in the middle and at the end of the school year – ten winners were drawn, and they too won 1,000 Schillings each in new banknotes. The principle here was "practice makes perfect".

Two thousand people questioned in an opinion poll showed a very high degree of recognition of banknote security features, particularly the watermark and the security thread. This was not the only test of the information campaign's heightening of public awareness, however. Two hopeful criminals made some primitive, handcoloured photocopies of 500 Schilling notes and tried to use them to pay a taxidriver, who at once recognised them as counterfeit. The perpetrators fled. . . .

Australia: Public information

Before the first notes of the Australian decimal currency note series ($1, $2, $10 and $20) were issued in 1966, a great deal of discussion took place within the Reserve Bank of Australia. It was necessary to decide how far the public should be informed of the new notes' security features. But would a fully detailed explanation of these features stimulate prospective forgers into activity, or deter them through people's heightened interest in the security aspects of notes? In the end a restricted approach was adopted: the public was informed about the primary defence features only.

The Bank publicised the designs of the new notes two weeks before their issue. The designs were described in detail in the press and on television. The portraits on the notes were given particularly close attention, and short biographies of their subjects were provided. The sizes of the notes and the basic colours used in each denomination were described, and publication of black and white photographs of the new currency was authorised, provided they did not form part of an advertisement and were of a substantially different size to that of actual notes. People were encouraged to be on their guard against accepting counterfeits by identifying the basic security features, as follows:

(a) The intaglio-printed features of the notes had the characteristic embossed "feel" when the fingers were run across the surface, arising from the raised film of ink.

(b) The background designs consisted of very clearly defined patterns of thick and thin lines.

(c) The banknote paper had a characteristic texture and special crispness. It contained a watermark portrait of Captain Cook and an embedded metal thread running vertically near the centre of each note.

Forged $10 notes nevertheless appeared within a few months, and the Governor of the Bank announced a reward of up to $10,000 for information leading to the arrest and conviction of people producing, uttering or unlawfully possessing forged Australian notes. Banks and businesses were sent a reference card listing the numbers of known counterfeit notes, as an aid to the prompt detection of distributors.

Reference card

The $5 note was issued in 1967, the $50 note in 1973, and the $100 note in 1984, at which time the $1 note was replaced by a coin. The $50 and $100 notes both bore a continuous watermark of Captain Cook, in contrast to the single portrait in the lower denominations.

The press release for the $100 note, as before, provided biographical information on portraiture, and details of size, colours, and readily identifiable security features. These again included the raised intaglio printing of the portraits, numerals and illustrative material, the clearly defined line patterns in the background printing, the range of colours, the characteristic feel and crispness of banknote paper and the presence of a watermark and thread.

Again, the widest possible media coverage of the release of the new $100 note was mounted in all Australian states, and the branches of all banks and other financial institutions displayed illustrative posters.

The experience gained during the decimal currency issue confirmed the view that banknote issuers can best prevent major forgeries by doing everything possible to familiarise the public with the appearance and primary security features of any new currency note.

Poster describing the 1984 $100 note

79

MILESTONES AND HIGHLIGHTS

AUSTRALIA

AUSTRIA

CHINA

ENGLAND

GERMANY

SPAIN

SWEDEN

UNITED STATES

Banknote of 1824 for 20 Spanish dollars

AUSTRALIA

English copper penny of 1797 (obverse and reverse)

Captain James Cook

MILESTONES IN AUSTRALIAN BANKNOTE PRINTING

The first currencies

Although Australia is the oldest continent geologically, it was the last to be settled by Europeans.

Several discoveries were made along its northern and western coastlines during the seventeenth century, particularly by the Dutch, but no attempt was made to settle it until in 1770 James Cook approached the continent from the east and so discovered the more fertile eastern area, which he named 'New South Wales'. His landing opened the way to the annexation of Australia by Britain, and sixteen years later the British Government decided to establish a convict settlement in New South Wales. The first group of settlers left England in May 1787 in a fleet of ships under the leadership of Arthur Phillip, arriving at Sydney Cove eight months later.

Britain was in no position to supply the new settlement with enough coins at that time, as it was short of currency itself. Various coins were circulating in the colony, but their values were not standardised until 1800, when a selection of coins was made by proclamation to circulate as legal tender by metallic weight.

Silver Spanish dollar (eight reals)

"Holey-dollar" (five shillings)

Dump (fifteen pence)

Australia's first distinctive currency took the form of "holey-dollar" coins. These coins were the circulating Spanish dollars (eight reals) with the centres punched out. The trim of the larger, ring-shaped portion was counterstamped "five shillings – New South Wales 1813", and the centre portion or "dump" was stamped "fifteen pence". The original single coin thus became two, with a total value of six shillings and threepence.

Other coinage

To meet the extreme shortage of small change in the 1850s and early 1860s, many tradesmen issued their own pennies and halfpennies. These were not legal tender, but were tolerated by the authorities, and like the "proclamation coins" of 1800 circulated freely, further supplementing the inadequate supply of British coins.

Australia's first gold coins were struck at the Sydney branch of the Royal Mint in 1855. In 1872 a branch was established in Melbourne to process gold mined in Victoria, and in 1899 the Perth Mint became the third Australian mint to strike coins in gold. The first Australian silver and copper coinage was manufactured in Britain from 1910, but six years later the Mint's Melbourne branch took over the production.

Over the years many mints around the world have struck coins for Australia. Today, however, the Royal Australian Mint in Canberra is responsible for producing Australia's circulating coinage.

Obverse   *Reverse*

A typical tradesman's copper penny token

The role of the private banks

The first Australian paper currency was issued in New South Wales in 1802, in the form of promissory notes and store receipts. Forgeries were common, however, and in 1817 Governor Macquarie tried to get rid of the problem by authorising the newly formed Bank of New South Wales to issue banknotes. The earliest known notes are dated 1819. By the early 1820s, notes on issue ranged from 2s. 6d. to £5 and also included notes in denominations of Spanish dollars.

Promissory note of 1826

85

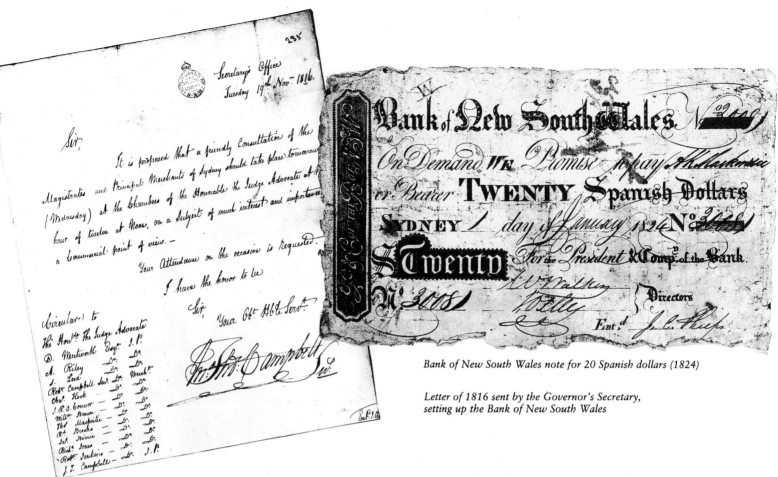

Bank of New South Wales note for 20 Spanish dollars (1824)

Letter of 1816 sent by the Governor's Secretary,
setting up the Bank of New South Wales

Between 1830 and 1870 many new banks sprang up, especially after the discoveries of gold during the 1850s. Each bank issued its own notes; notes were particularly popular on the goldfields, because they were easier to handle (and conceal) than gold.

Notes issued by private banks (details)

Chinese characters appeared on some notes at the time of the Gold Rush

86

Issue of the Colonial Bank of Australasia, Melbourne, ca 1886;
the miner with his shovel was a common sight on the goldfields

Many of these early banks were short-lived, vanishing during the economic crises of the 1840s and the major collapse of 1892–93. These failures highlighted the need for a central banking authority to assume the power to issue banknotes.

The end of the nineteenth century saw a move towards a federation of the six Australian States, culminating in the formation of the Commonwealth of Australia in 1901. The new constitution gave the Commonwealth Parliament the power in part to legislate for currency coinage and legal tender, non-state banking and the issue of paper money.

In 1910, the Commonwealth Treasury asked the banks to estimate their note requirements. Although the private banks still had the right to issue notes at that time, it was effectively removed by the imposition of a ten per cent tax on every note they issued or re-issued.

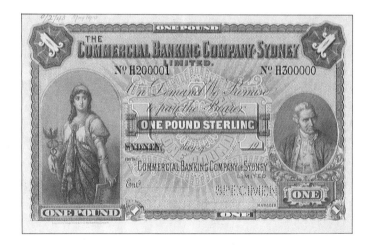

Detail of a £1 note of 1900

£1 note issued by
the Commercial Banking
Company of Sydney Limited

87

The Treasury's lack of facilities prevented it from printing the necessary number of notes quickly enough, however, and the Commonwealth therefore arranged to buy the banks' own unsigned blank forms for overprinting. For three years overprinted notes from at least fifteen banks were issued; the superscription of these notes was undertaken at the Treasury Building, Melbourne.

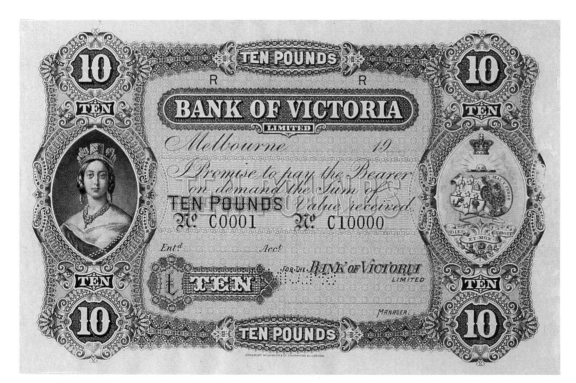

£10 note issued by the Bank of Victoria in 1910 and detail of overprinting (right)

Commonwealth Government stamp and banknote printers

Detail of bank and Commonwealth notes

In 1909, J. B. Cooke was appointed Australia's first Stamp Printer, and took up his post at the Old Kings (Customs) Warehouse in Melbourne. In October 1912 T. S. Harrison, newly arrived from England, set up note printing operations in another part of the same building. Machinery was acquired, and the printing of Australian currency notes began in the following year. On Cooke's retirement in 1918, the Stamp Printing Branch was abolished, and Harrison became the Stamp and Note Printer.

The father of Australian note printing, Thomas Samuel Harrison

The Old Kings (Customs) Warehouse, Melbourne

The numbering of the first Australian note in 1913

The ceremony following the numbering of the first note

Stamps issued by the Commonwealth Government Stamp Printer

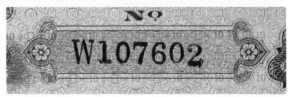

Examples of numbering

The 1913 printing of £1 notes was too small to satisfy demand and a hastily designed emergency issue of the same value was introduced in 1914. The Australian public christened it the "rainbow-issue", because of its rainbow colour effect. The simple printing method used made the notes relatively easy to copy, however, and they were withdrawn early in 1915.

Until 1915, when Australia abandoned the gold standard, Australian notes could be converted into gold coin on demand. The nation returned to a form of gold standard in 1925 but, although Australian notes still bore the Treasurer of Australia's promise to redeem them in gold on demand, in practice the notes remained non-convertible. The undertaking to redeem notes in gold coin disappeared at last in 1932, leaving the provision that notes should circulate as legal tender.

*The emergency £1 note of 1914,
front and back*

£1 note of 1913, front

Commonwealth Bank of Australia

The Commonwealth Bank was established in 1911 as banker to the Commonwealth Government; an Act of 1924 also gave it the responsibility for the note issue, previously borne by the Treasury. The same year saw the setting up of its note-printing and issuing branches in separate buildings on the same site, in the Melbourne suburb of Fitzroy.

*Guilloche from the
1934 ten-shilling note*

£1 note of 1938 series, front and back

The Reserve Bank of Australia

£5 note of 1960, front

Under the provisions of the Reserve Bank Act of 1959, the Reserve Bank of Australia took over the responsibility for the Commonwealth Bank of Australia's central banking functions, including note printing; security printing activities continued to be carried out at the Fitzroy premises until 1981, when they were transferred to Craigieburn, near Melbourne.

The site of the new Note Printing Works covers an area of 26.3 hectares and is bounded by a double security fence. Production is carried on in a four-storied reinforced concrete building flanked by large landscaped gardens; all the printing and finishing operations and strongrooms are on the same level — there are no basements, as the foundations rest on bedrock. Security guards protect the complex round the clock, supported by a range of highly sophisticated electronic security and surveillance devices.

The Note Printing Works at Craigieburn

HIGHLIGHTS OF AUSTRALIAN BANKNOTE DESIGN

In 1913 the Commonwealth of Australia designed and printed a banknote in Australia for the first time – the first of a series that ranged in value from ten shillings through to £1,000.

Although the design had an Australian flavour, there were obvious influences from the U.K.-based firm of Bradbury Wilkinson & Co. Ltd, who had given assistance with security graphics and engraving expertise. European style guilloche patterns formed borders and corner rosettes, and the background patterns were printed by the letterpress process by two passes through a single colour Miehle press. The design was simple and easy to identify and the intaglio print produced on Hoe flat bed machines was of high quality. There were no engraved portraits and no watermarks, however, so the notes' security value was not high.

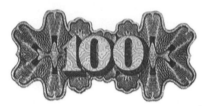

Examples of corner rosettes

1770	*James Cook, commanding the* Endeavour *and accompanied by the botanist and scientist Joseph Banks ($5 note portrait), sails down the eastern coast of Australia and formally claims possession of New South Wales for Britain.*
1788	*First European settlement of Australia. The First Fleet led by Captain Arthur Phillip arrives at Sydney Cove ($10 commemorative note motif).*
	The French navigator, La Perouse, appears unexpectedly at Botany Bay soon after the arrival of the First Fleet.
1790	*John MacArthur ($2 note portrait) arrives from England with the Second Fleet and pioneers sheep breeding in Australia.*
1813	*The "holey-dollar", Australia's first distinctive coin, is produced from a Spanish dollar.*
1814	*The only convict to appear on an Australian banknote, Francis Greenway ($10 note portrait) is transported to Australia; an architect and stonemason, he later designed some of Australia's finest early buildings.*
1817	*Australia's first bank, The Bank of New South Wales, is established and authorised to issue banknotes.*
1840	*Transportation of convicts to New South Wales is ended.*
1851	*The Gold Rush: gold discoveries in Victoria and New South Wales attract an influx of prospectors.*
1861	*John Tebbutt ($100 note portrait) discovers the first of his two comets (only twelve were discovered in the whole of the nineteenth century, and a crater on the moon has been named after Tebbutt).*
	First running of the Melbourne Cup for thoroughbred racehorses.
1880	*Ned Kelly, the notorious bushranger and bankrobber, is brought to trial.*

John MacArthur

The Commonwealth of Australia's first banknote, issued in 1913

Intaglio-printed portrait

Clearly, one way of improving security was to use the services of specialist engravers and printers. These experts soon added a range of security features to Australian banknote designs.

The designers of the 1923 series of notes acknowledged the value of an engraved portrait. Watermarks were introduced too, and more guilloche patterns adorned the notes. From a security viewpoint, the 1923 designs parallelled those of many European notes of the time.

Continuous watermark

The Australian Federal Parliament building in Canberra

1887	Australian soprano Nellie Melba, one of the world's great prima donnas, makes her operatic debut in Brussels. Henry Lawson ($10 note portrait) publishes his first poem.
1894	Aviation pioneer Lawrence Hargrave ($20 note portrait) flies to a height of nearly five metres with the aid of four box-kites.
1895	Poet A. B. (Banjo) Paterson writes the words of "Waltzing Matilda", Australia's unofficial national song.
1901	Federation of Australia. The Australian Commonwealth Government is formed and the flag chosen by a public contest. William Farrer ($2 note portrait) develops new early-maturing and more drought-resistant wheat variety.
1907	Geologist and Antarctic explorer Douglas Mawson ($100 note portrait) visits the Antarctic for the first time with Ernest Shackleton's expedition.
1910	John Duigan flies the first Australian-built aeroplane at Spring Plains, Victoria.
1913	Australia's first distinctive banknotes are printed in Melbourne.
1917	Completion of the transcontinental railway.
1920	Australia's international airline, Qantas, is founded.

The Qantas logo

The 1923 series £1 note, front and back

Bas-relief portraits

By the early 1950s, a new series of notes was required. The Commonwealth Bank decided to combine artistic talent with security, and commissioned two of Australia's best-known artists, the painter Napier Waller and the sculptor Les Bowles, to assist with the new designs. Bowles' influence on the engravers is evident in the *bas-relief* portraits carried by some of the notes – a feature not often found in European designs. There was much more intaglio than on past notes, and the Australian influence on the designs was far stronger. Background patterns were letterpress, with a combination of micro-lettering and guilloche patterns.

1921	*Edith Cowan, first woman member of any Australian Parliament, is elected to the Western Australian Parliament.*
1924	*Parliament transfers responsibility for the note issue from the Treasury to the Commonwealth Bank. Banknote printing is transferred to the Bank's premises in Fitzroy, near Melbourne.*
1927	*Australia's Federal Parliament building is opened in Canberra.*
1928	*Charles Kingsford-Smith and Charles Ulm make the first flight across the Pacific in the aircraft* Southern Cross.
1932	*Completion of the Sydney Harbour Bridge.*
1942	*Howard Florey (Lord Florey, $50 note portrait) perfects the purification of penicillin which has been responsible for the saving of thousands of lives.*
1949	*Ian Clunies Ross ($50 note portrait), veterinarian and parasitologist, is appointed chairman of the Commonwealth Scientific and Industrial Research Organization.*
1951	*ANZUS Treaty is signed for the mutual defence of Australia, New Zealand and the United States.*
1954	*First tour of Australia by a reigning British monarch (Queen Elizabeth II).*

Howard Florey

The 1953 series £1 note, front and back

A new approach to design

In 1963 the Australian Government decided to change to decimal currency. The Governor of the Reserve Bank of Australia, Dr. H. C. Coombs, met this challenge with a determination that the new series should not only use state-of-the-art technology, but also be characteristically Australian.

Rough drawings were commissioned from several distinguished Australian commercial designers and, after much discussion, the roughs from the industrial designer Gordon Andrews were adopted for development into a family of banknote designs.

Not only were Andrews' designs as distinctively Australian as Dr. Coombs had wished, but the strong background colours he used were novel – his bright greens, browns, golds, oranges and reds were a complete breakaway from the conventionally subtle tones of banknotes of the time.

Detail of the $5 note (front) showing the strong colours used in the background tint

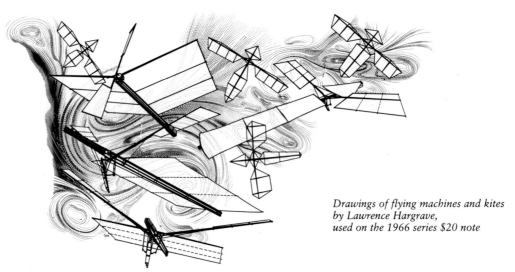

Drawings of flying machines and kites by Lawrence Hargrave, used on the 1966 series $20 note

Sydney Opera House

1956	*Television broadcasts begin in Australia. XVIth modern Olympic Games held in Melbourne.*
1966	*Decimal currency comes into circulation in Australia.*
1973	*Sydney Opera House opened.*
1981	*Production of Australia's banknotes transferred to a new security printing complex at Craigieburn near Melbourne.*

$10 note of the 1966 series, back and front

$50 note of 1973, back

The immigrant ship Waverley *(detail from the back of the $5 note)*

Multicoloured detail from the $50 note

The engravings were deliberately prepared with strongly contrasting highlights and shadows. The depth of background colour Andrews wanted could not be achieved with the recognised techniques for guilloche patterns, medallion rulings and fine line printing. Together with the bank's artists he completely reversed the accepted methods of the day, using boldly defined patterns with overprinted shapes in place of myriads of fine lines in several colours – a total innovation in security graphics.

The latest Kämpf geometric lathe and three Giori Intagliocolour and two Simultan machines were installed to produce the new designs. The result was a series of banknotes – $1, $2, $10 and $20 – that was indeed distinctively Australian, and which had a level of security at least equal to that of other currencies.

Three further denominations were later added to the series – $5 in 1967, $50 in 1973 and $100 in 1984. The $50 and $100 denominations incorporate three-colour intaglio printing on both back and front, and multiple watermarks in positive and negative format. The $100 note also carries moiré-inducing patterns, developed to counter the oncoming threat of the colour copier.

1983	*Australia wins the America's Cup – the first country to defeat the United States in this event.*
1984	*"Advance Australia Fair" is adopted as the official National Anthem.*
1988	*Australia's Bicentennial year, commemorated by the $10 plastic-based banknote incorporating an optically variable device as a security feature.*

$100 note of 1984, front and back

1966: Ethnic art in banknote design

The first banknote to use the work of Aboriginal artists was the 1966 $1 note. The design for the back of the note included details from Aboriginal rock drawings and carvings of reptiles and animals, as well as of Aboriginal hunters and fishermen. It was based on a bark painting by Malangi, an Aborigine living at Milingimbi Mission on an island off Arnhem Land in Northern Australia. Aboriginal influences were evident too in the design for the stylised Australian coat of arms on the front of the note.

This note was replaced by a coin in May 1984.

Aboriginal influence in the design of the Australian coat of arms

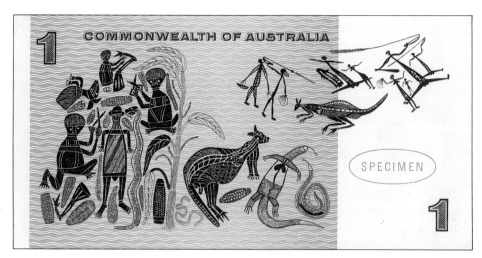

Aboriginal figures on the back of the 1966 series $1 note

*Australia's first
$1 coin*

1967: The female portrait

The 1967 $5 note was the first Australian banknote to carry a portrait of a woman other than the ruling monarch. Caroline Chisholm was chosen for this honour because of the way in which she encouraged women and families to migrate from England to Australia. In 1841, she established the Female Immigrants Home in which girls newly arrived from England could live until they found work.

Caroline Chisholm (1808–1877)

1974: The Commonwealth of Australia becomes Australia

The name "Commonwealth of Australia" was introduced in 1901 to describe the federated Australian states, but by 1974 it was no longer thought appropriate and the Prime Minister of the time, the Right Honourable E. G. Whitlam, decided that the phrase should be amended to "Australia" in all official descriptions. The amended Australian banknotes thus became consistent with the circulating coinage, which already bore the word "Australia".

1966:

1974:

NATIONAL

Geniefst die volle Dividende vom Jahre *1820* an

vom Jahre 1868
mit fl. 135 geleistet

Nro *6.*

Mit Coupons No *28628* bis Ende 1830

Mit Coupons No *28628* bisEnde1850

Mit Coupons No *28628* bisEnde18

ACTIE

der privil. oesterreich. National-B

Die privilegirte oesterreichische National-Bank erkläret hiermit, *Herr Ludwig van Beethoven.* oder, dieser Urkunde, in Folge der geleisteten statutenmäfsigen Einlage, au Statt haben kann, Eigenthümer der Act... Fol. *2099.* Nro. daher an allen Rechten Theil zu nehmen *hat* , welche den Actionä reichischen National-Bank, vermöge ihrer allerhöchst genehmigter zustehen und zustehen werden.

Wien am *13.ᵗ Juli* 18*19.*

Mit Coupons No *28628* bis Ende 1870 und Talon.

Neue Actie angesprochen

Consign. № 5392

790

Folio 3099

MitCoupons
№ 28628
bisEnde 1840

mäfsige Inhaber
e ein Zuzahlung
orden ist, und
vilegirten oester-
und Privilegien,

Berger

Nolar

AUSTRIA

Share certificate issued by the Privilegirte Oesterreichische National-Bank,
registered in the name of Ludwig van Beethoven

MILESTONES IN AUSTRIAN BANKNOTE PRINTING

Austrian banknotes are printed today by the National Bank, but their history began in the early eighteenth century, long before the Privilegirte Oesterreichische National-Bank, the present Bank's lineal predecessor, was founded.

Ten-Gulden Banco-Zettel of 1762

The first security features

The Wiener-Stadt-Banco, founded in 1705, issued the first Austrian banknotes, which were dated 1 July, 1762. They were printed by the two colour letterpress process, and carried blind-tooled (embossed) coats of arms in the upper left and lower right corners. Like later issues from the Wiener-Stadt-Banco, they were also elaborately ornamented with several different styles of calligraphy on each denomination, together with handwritten serial numbers – all designed to deter potential forgers. At the time, it was not easy to duplicate a two colour letterpress print with various founts: the lithographic and photographic processes relied on by twentieth-century forgers had not been invented. Moreover, embossing was only for the unusually intrepid, since the very use of embossing tools was punishable by death after 1803.

Punishment warning printed on banknotes

The hand-produced features were also important. The authorities of the time were convinced that hand numbering together with a handwritten signature and paraph were safeguards against counterfeiting because, they assumed, the clerk who signed the notes would be able to distinguish his own signature from a forgery.

The paper

The role of paper in deterring the counterfeiter was probably appreciated by banknote printers before the end of the eighteenth century. The series dated 1 November, 1784 was the first to be printed on watermarked paper.

Later developments included better-quality paper and watermarks (these could be made to produce an effect of light and shade when held up to the light) and the addition of fibres to the pulp to foil counterfeiters.

The first register

The last series from the Wiener-Stadt-Banco, dated 1 June 1806, pioneered a novel printing technique: the "completely new and unprecedented double and counterpressure method" invented by the printer Johann Ferdinand Edler von Schönfeld.

For the first time, the reverse of the notes was printed as well as the front and, when the note was held up to the light, individual portions of the front design could be seen to be in register with the design on the back. This security feature survives today (in a technically improved version) in the register ornament on the latest series of Austrian banknotes (page 15).

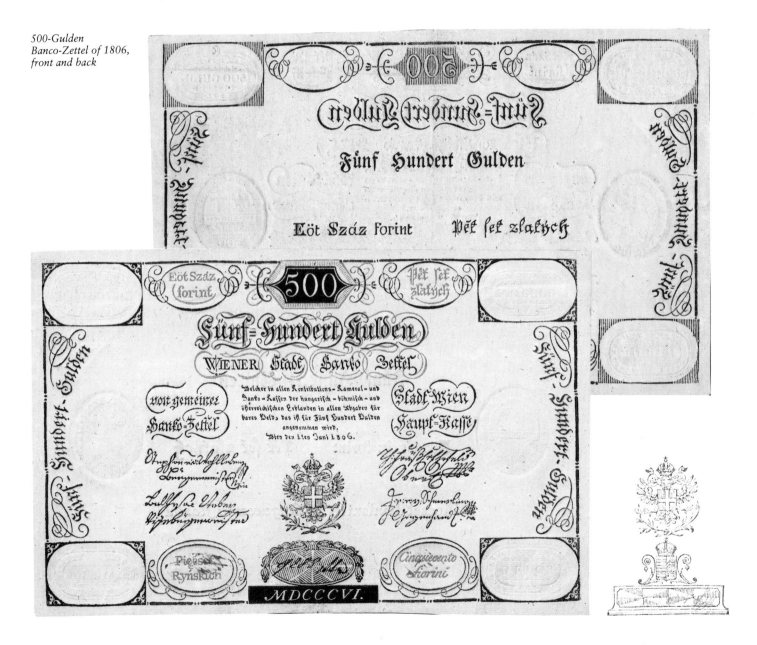

*500-Gulden
Banco-Zettel of 1806,
front and back*

*An example of
Degen's "dual" technique*

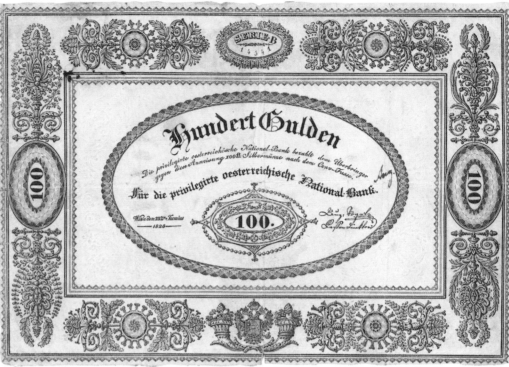

100-Gulden banknote of 1825

The Degen effect

Jakob Degen was an Austrian inventor whose exceptionally fertile brain was combined with unusual ingenuity. He developed a guilloche machine as early as 1810; this "wheel cutting and stamp engraving machine" allowed the production of exact line patterns, each derived from a specific mathematical formula, and over the years innumerable notes around the world came to carry Degen's guilloche patterns as security features. He also invented or improved a whole range of banknote-printing equipment, including a numbering machine and a stamping machine that could produce extremely intricate blind blocked or embossed stamps.

All these innovations were used in the production of the series of Austrian notes dated 23 June 1825, which were in circulation in the 1830s. They were designed by the National Bank's own artist, Johann Baptist Danzinger, and printed under Degen's supervision by means of yet another Degen invention, the "dual technique", which provided higher quality and security. Degen's idea was to separate the guilloche printing unit for a single note into several precisely fitting movable parts, each of which could be inked in a different colour. The individual parts were reassembled for printing and the resulting notes had multicoloured guilloches with an unusually precise colour registration.

And still another innovation, a new ink that was not transferable to stone, was developed by August Richard, the Bank's lithographer; this provided yet another safeguard against forgery.

Intaglio printing

Perhaps the single most important development in the printing of banknotes in Austria was the introduction of siderography (the steel engraving system) in the 1840s. Intaglio printing, the security feature which the Bank still emphasises in its brochures on the latest series of notes, is based on siderography.

50-Gulden banknote of 1841 (details)

Eroticism...

Steel engraving was introduced to banknote printing at the initiative of Franz von Salzmann, chief clerk at the Bank and an expert in the science and practice of note printing. He recorded his experience in a paper entitled "Collected Observations for the Expedient Production of Banknotes and other Credit Paper to Prevent Counterfeiting".

Among Salzmann's suggestions was the use of erotic illustration to deter potential forgers. In his paper he proposed that "such a measure of nudity [should] prevail as is in keeping with decorum" (in addition to large, expressive portrait heads).

His logic was that his lightly clad lovelies "make such a lasting impression even on any common man that he would immediately notice any deviation from the true likeness". Sigmund Freud, was not to be born for another nineteen years. . . .

...and art

The new notes, dated 1 January, 1841, which were engraved in Vienna by Peter Fendi, the Biedermeier painter, and by the copper engravers of the Vienna Academy of Fine Arts. The designs bore little resemblance to their predecessors, with their elaborate calligraphy and ornate guilloche patterns.

Alongside the portrait medallions of a "spirit of Austria", naked cherubs and young women in diaphanous draperies disported themselves across the notes, together with a scantily dressed Aquarius who symbolised the river Danube. Perhaps fewer eyebrows were raised at the architectural motifs that also appeared for the first time, including the Äußere Burgtor (completed in 1824) and a view of Vienna with St Stephen's Cathedral.

In later years these peaceful images were increasingly superseded by symbols of imperial power, such as lions and swords, but warlike symbols such as cannons and cannonballs, favoured by the Italian banknotes of the time, were never found on Austrian notes.

Symbols of Imperial power

Ten-Gulden note of 1858

Von Salzmann's mistake

Franz von Salzmann had assured the bank management that the introduction of siderographic techniques would guarantee the inimitability of the new notes. But he was wrong.

Salzmann had underestimated the ingenuity of forgers who were helped both by lithography and, most importantly, the newly invented photography. Against these eroticism alone, it seemed, was not enough. Nor did prospective forgers seem alarmed by the written warning on the notes that counterfeiting was a punishable offence.

So the guilloche patterns, which had all but disappeared from the banknotes of 1 January, 1841, reappeared at the end of the 1850s as an undertint of a different colour from the main design, as a precaution against forgery by photography.

The dualistic series

Ten-Gulden note of the dual monarchy (1880)

In 1867 the dual monarchy of Austria and Hungary was established, and Hungary could no longer accept a specifically Austrian National Bank. But the two governments were not able to settle their differences until 1878, when the Privilegirte Oesterreichische National-Bank became the Oesterreichisch-ungarische Bank (the Austro-Hungarian Bank).

The new bank's first series of notes, dated 1 May, 1880, clearly reflects the effort not to favour either of the Danubian monarchies at the expense of the other. One side of the note is in German and the other Hungarian, but the designs on the two sides were otherwise identical.

The design for the ten-Gulden note turned dualism in design into a printing advantage: it included a girl's portrait on both sides. When the note was held up to the light, the identical portraits were exactly complementary – in theory. Unfortunately, the presses of the time did not always achieve a perfect register between the prints on the front and back of the note. When the ten-gulden note was issued, a contemporary newspaper article commented that the lines along the girl's nose sometimes appeared side by side!

Heliography

Although it had originally been intended that the 1880 series would be printed by the intaglio process, the tradition was for some reason abandoned. Instead the notes were printed by heliography, a technique for engraving plates by photography, developed in 1867 by Emil Mariot at the Vienna Military Geographic Institute. Various theories for the departure from the intaglio process have been advanced, but the real reason remains a mystery. It may be a political one: that the designers could not decide which side of the note – the German or the Hungarian – should be printed in intaglio, for at the time, the printers had no experience of intaglio printing on both sides. Indeed, when the first Kronen banknotes were intaglio-printed on both sides twenty years later, they looked curiously flat.

The 1880 series also pioneered the use of security inks that were difficult to reproduce. The development of new inks and new applications for them have remained important weapons in the printer's armoury against the counterfeiter.

Art nouveau

*Detail from a design
by Koloman Moser*

Design by Gustav Klimt

In the 1890s the dual monarchy of Austria and Hungary introduced a new currency, based on the Krone, and the issue of new banknotes followed.

Designs were produced by Rudolf Rössler, who studied at the Academy, and also by Gustav Klimt, one of the best known of Austrian painters. None of the Klimt's designs was actually printed, but his influence is obvious in Rössler's ten-, 20- and 50-Kronen notes, which were issued around the turn of the century.

*100-Kronen note of 1912, with
a protective grid across the "ideal" portrait*

Sketch by Josef Pfeiffer

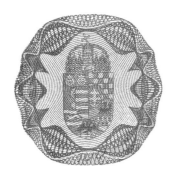

"Iridescent" printing

The copperplate engraver Ferdinand Schirnböck, another product of the Academy, introduced copperplate engraving for banknote printing and was also responsible for the replacement of allegorical scenes by contemporary portraits. Schirnböck engraved the 100-Kronen note dated 2 January, 1910, which was designed by Koloman Moser, the Jugendstil artist. The note was widely forged, however, and just two years later, a new note had to be issued. It included two new security features: a protective grid around the intaglio "ideal portrait" of a girl, and a composite background produced by printing several motifs over one another, so that each corner of the note was a different colour.

The high quality of the notes designed by the Bank's artist Josef Pfeiffer (born in Reichenberg, Bohemia, in 1864 and died in Vienna in 1915) reflects the expertise of the Securities Printing Works and the technical improvements to presses and guilloche machines made by its staff. These included Nadherny, the head of the works, and the technician Maly – who gave their names to the Nadherny–Maly system, an intaglio press and guilloche machine – and Gustav Tauschek, who worked as a clerk at the Bank in the 1920s and contributed to the improvement of a guilloche machine. This ingenious inventor later became famous for registering more than 200 patents while working for IBM, the multinational manufacturer of office machines and computers.

Detail of the 1,000,000-Kronen banknote of 1924 (unissued)

The first Republic

The hyperinflation that followed the end of the dual monarchy inevitably had a deleterious effect on the paper and print quality of banknotes. But from 1925 onwards, the notes issued by the newly founded Austrian National Bank to accompany the new Schilling currency recovered the high standard to which Austrians had been accustomed.

The Bank continued to develop and improve its techniques. A portrait watermark was used for the first time in the margin of the 1,000 Schilling note dated 2 January, 1930, and was secured by means of a fine screed of regular, unbroken lines. Background printing by the Orloff process was introduced in the mid-1930s. Developed in the nineteenth century by the Russian Ivan Orloff, this technique allows the hairline register of the differently coloured line patterns. It was used for the first time to print the 20-Schilling note of 2 February, 1946.

1000-Schilling banknote of 1930 (front) and its portrait watermark

116

Intaglio printing department at the National Bank (about 1920)

Ten-Schilling banknote of 1933, back

Larger intaglio presses, capable of accommodating uncut sheets of twelve or even eighteen notes, were also introduced, and used to print the ten-Schilling notes dated 2 January, 1933.

20-Schilling note of 1946, back; the background was printed by the Orloff process

Detail of Orloff print

The security thread

The first Austrian banknote to incorporate a security thread was the 100-Schilling issue of 3 January, 1949. It was designed by Erhard Amadeus-Dier, the painter and graphic artist, who initially followed Salzmann's tradition in his design. The Danube nymph on the back of the 1949 note is among the loveliest of his works. The choice of Dier, whose love of the baroque was well known, to design the series is interesting: his themes are a far cry from life in post-war Austria under Allied occupation.

The note was also the first to be printed by the iris intaglio method, where the rainbow effect of the intaglio print on the back of the note is produced by the iris inking of the plates. The new generation of multicolour intaglio presses introduced in the early 1950s made the same effect possible without iris inking, however. New guilloche machines also drew guilloches in greater variety, more precisely and much faster than before – and the new multicolour presses could print them in different colours.

100-Schilling note of 1949, back

Simultaneous printing

The first note to be produced by the simultaneous printing technique: the 1956 20-Schilling note (back)

Supersimultan printing press

The development of simultaneous background printing by the dry offset method owed much to the staff of the National Bank. Dry offset printing began in the 1930s, but its development was held back because of the lack of suitable printing plates. In 1954, however, the National Bank's printing works overcame this problem and by 1956 the Bank became the first in the world to install a simultaneous press to print both sides of banknote paper at once. The first press, built in Mödling near Vienna, had five separate printing units: two for the front of the paper and three for the back.

Growing demands for accuracy and efficiency have led to continual improvements. The super-simultaneous press now in use has eight separate units (four for each side) and electronic controls. The high standards of accuracy of these machines in registering the printing forms are of crucial importance for printing the transparent register ornament that is still a key security feature of Austrian banknotes.

HIGHLIGHTS OF AUSTRIAN BANKNOTE DESIGN

The first home of the National Bank in Vienna, opened in 1823

Aquarius

100-Gulden banknote dated 1 January, 1841

The series was designed by the Biedermeier painter and copper engraver Peter Fendi (1796–1842 in Vienna), and was in circulation from 1842 to 1852; it was part of the first series to be printed by the siderographic system (steel engraving).

The notes, printed on watermarked paper, had a completely new design: the previous calligraphy was replaced by allegorical representations of cherubs and portraits of "Austria". The note also carried an architectural motif, used here for the first time: the Aeußere Burgtor, completed in 1824.

1814–15	*Congress of Vienna and establishment of a new order in Europe after Napoleon's defeat.*
1816	*Salzburg becomes part of Austria.*
	Foundation in Vienna of the Privilegirte Oesterreichische National-Bank, the forerunner of the Austrian National Bank.
1818	*Silent night sung for the first time in Oberndorf near Salzburg.*
1819	*The composer Ludwig van Beethoven (born 1770 in Bonn, Germany) buys eight shares of the Privilegirte Oesterreichische National-Bank.*
1825	*Josef Ressel (born in Chrudim, Bohemia) invents the marine screw propeller.*
1828	*The classical romantic composer Franz Schubert (born in Vienna in 1797) dies in Vienna.*
1832	*The first European long distance railway, the horse drawn train from Linz via Freistadt to Budweis (Budejovice), begins service.*
1835	*Josef Lanner (born in 1801 in Vienna) makes the Viennese Waltz the nineteenth century's favourite dance.*
1841	*Otto Wagner, one of the most renowned Austrian architects, born in Vienna.*

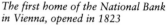

Franz Schubert

120

A design by Peter Fendi (not used)

50-Kronen banknote dated 2 January, 1902

The note was designed by the genre painter Rudolf Rössler (1864–1954) and engraved by Ferdinand Schirnböck (1849–1930), who engraved many Austrian and foreign banknotes and stamps and who trained other Austrian engravers. The paper has no watermark. The note was in circulation from 1902 to 1919.

In accordance with the dual structure of the Austro-Hungarian monarchy, the face and reverse of the note have the same motif, consisting of two idealised female figures, one of them with a sickle in her hand, the other holding a closed book.

While the inscription on the Hungarian side of the note is in Hungarian only, that on the German side gives the denomination also in the other eight languages of the Austro-Hungarian monarchy, namely Czech, Polish, Ruthenian (Ukrainian), Italian, Slovene, Croat, Serbian and Romanian.

The 10-Kronen note of the same series, dated 31 March, 1900, is also illustrated.

Detail of the Austro-Hungarian bank-share

1842	*First concert performance by the Vienna Philharmonic Orchestra.*
1847	*Ignaz Semmelweis (born in Buda in 1818) discovers the cause of childbed fever.*
1848	*Lajos Kossuth (born in 1802) becomes the leader of the Magyar insurrection. Beginning of the struggle for Hungarian national independence.*
1849	*The rebellion against the Habsburgs in Vienna and Hungary is crushed with armed support from Russia.*
1854	*Opening of the Semmering railway, the first mountain railway in Europe.*
1859	*Austria is defeated by the Kingdom of Sardinia and by France.*
1866	*Austria defeated by Prussia; the war is partly financed by Austrian government issues of paper money. Peter Mitterhofer (born in Partschins, South Tyrol, in 1822) constructs a typewriter.*
1867	*Compromise between Austria and Hungary: the formation of the dual monarchy.*
1869	*Opening of the Suez Canal – plans by Alois Ritter V. Negrelli, who had died in Vienna in 1858, were used to construct it.*
1878	*The conversion of the Privilegirte Oesterreichische National-Bank into the Austro-Hungarian Bank – a late consequence of the Compromise of 1867.*
1892	*Introduction of the Kronen currency (gold standard) in Austria: 2 Kronen = 1 Gulden, 1 Krone = 100 Heller.*
1898	*Beginning of the Art Nouveau period.*
1900	*Richard Kuhn, who revolutionised biochemistry and was awarded the Nobel prize, born in Vienna.*

SERIE 1359

Die Oesterreichisch-ungarische Bank zahlt gegen diese Banknote bei ihren Hauptanstalten in Wien und Budapest sofort auf Verlangen

Fünfzig Kronen

in gesetzlichem Metallgelde.

Wien, 2. Jänner 1902.

Oesterreichisch-ungarische Bank.

Generalrath. Gouverneur. Generalsekretär.

DIE NACHMACHUNG DER BANKNOTEN WIRD GESETZLICH BESTRAFT.

PADESÁT KORUN · PIĘĆDZIESIĄT KORON · CINQUANTA CORONE
PETDESET KRON · PEDESET KRUNA · ПЕДЕСЕТ КРУНА · CINCIZECI COROANE

Die Oesterreichisch-ungarische Bank zahlt gegen diese Banknote bei ihren Hauptanstalten in Wien und Budapest sofort auf Verlangen

Zehn Kronen

in gesetzlichem Metallgelde.   Wien, 31. März 1900.

Oesterreichisch-ungarische Bank.

Generalrath. Gouverneur. Generalsekretär.

DIE NACHMACHUNG DER BANKNOTEN WIRD GESETZLICH BESTRAFT.

DESET KORUN · DZIESIĘĆ KORON · ДЕСЯТЬ КОРОН · DIECI CORONE
DESET KRON · DESET KRUNA · ДЕСЕТ КРУНА · ZECE COROANE

DIE NACHMACHUNG DER BANKNOTEN WIRD GESETZLICH BESTRAFT.

100-Kronen banknote dated 2 January, 1910

Motif of the "Wiener Werkstätte"

This is a particularly beautiful note, designed by Koloman ("Kolo") Moser (1868–1918 in Vienna), portrait, genre and landscape painter as well as graphic artist. He was a founding member of the Vienna Sezession and co-founder of the Wiener Werkstätte.

The note was engraved by Ferdinand Schirnböck. The banknote was in circulation only between 1910 and 1915; it was extensively forged, and was replaced by the 100-Kronen note of 2 January, 1912.

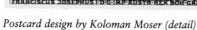

Postcard design by Koloman Moser (detail)

1903	Foundation of the "Wiener Werkstätte" by Josef Hoffmann and Kolo Moser (Vienna becomes the centre of a new arts and crafts style).
1904	Conclusion of the "entente cordiale" between France and England (against Germany and Austria).
1905	Bertha von Suttner (born in Prague in 1843) receives the Nobel peace prize.
1910	The Austro-Hungarian Bank's gold reserves reach a record level of over 410,000 kg.
1911	The founder of the German Peace Society, Alfred Fried (born in Vienna in 1864) is awarded the Nobel peace prize (together with T.M.C. Asser).
1912	Viktor Kaplan (born in Mürzzuschlag in Styria in 1876) invents the Kaplan turbine.
1914	Robert Bárány (born in Vienna in 1876) receives the Nobel prize for physiology and medicine. June 28: the Austrian heir apparent, Archduke Franz Ferdinand, and his wife are assassinated in Sarajevo. Austria declares war on Serbia on July 28.
1915	Italy joins the war against Austria.
1916	Emperor Franz Josef I of Austria dies.
1918	End of World War I: defeat of the Central Powers, the Danube monarchy breaks apart. November 12: proclamation of the Republik Deutschösterreich. Deaths of Klimt, Schiele and Otto Wagner.
1919	Peace treaty of Saint-Germain-en-Laye, which contained provisions for the dissolution of the Austro-Hungarian Bank.

Sketch by Koloman Moser

Stamp commemorating the 80th birthday of Franz Joseph I, designed by Koloman Moser

1000-Kronen banknote dated 2 January, 1902

The note was designed by Rudolf Rössler, using a sketch of the so called "ideal portrait" by Heinrich Lefler (1863–1919 in Vienna), landscape, genre painter and graphic artist. After the collapse of the Austro-Hungarian monarchy following World War I, some of the successor states began to overprint the Austro-Hungarian Bank's notes. (This was originally part of the statistical monitoring of banknote circulation in states such as Yugoslavia, but later accompanied the introduction of new national currencies, as in Czechoslovakia.) As a result, the Austro-Hungarian Bank was instructed by the government of Deutschösterreich in March 1919 to overprint the new banknotes issued in Austria itself. This note was in circulation from 1919 to 1924.

500,000-Kronen banknote dated 20 September, 1922

This banknote, issued by the Austrian management of the Austro-Hungarian Bank in Vienna, was the largest Austrian denomination ever issued. After the introduction of the schilling currency in December 1924, 500,000 Kronen equalled 50 Schillings. The note remained in circulation until 1926.

The main motif on the front, a mother with three children, is by Karl Sterrer (1885–1972 in Vienna), portrait, genre, still life and landscape painter as well as graphic artist.

Typical art nouveau design
on 100,000 Kronen note (detail)

1920	*The Austrian Constitution is drawn up by Hans Kelsen. Austria becomes a member of the Geneva-based League of Nations.*
	The Salzburg Festival is held for the first time.
1922	*Inflation reaches its height. Loans made under the supervision of the League of Nations allow the Austrian currency to be stabilised.*
	Foundation of the Austrian National Bank.

Detail of back

10,000-Kronen banknote dated 2 January, 1924

The note, designed by Rudolf Junk using a portrait by Rudolf Rössler, was issued in connection with the introduction of the new schilling currency in 1925: 10,000 Kronen in paper money equalled one Schilling, 100 Kronen in paper money equalled one groschen (the new divisional coin).

After 1926 divisional coins were used for the one-Schilling denomination; the National Bank no longer issued banknotes in this denomination, and the note was withdrawn.

100-Schilling banknote dated 2 January, 1925

The first Schilling banknote of the new Austrian National Bank, founded in 1922, was in circulation from 1925 to 1929. The portrait was by Karl Sterrer. This banknote series, the first issued by the Austrian National Bank, was designed by Rudolf Junk. Some of the designs had originally been intended for Kronen banknotes.

Portraits by Karl Sterrer used on the note-series 1924—25

1923	Foundation of the International Criminal Police Organisation (Interpol) in Vienna. Among its responsibilities is the detection of counterfeit money.
1925	Schilling currency introduced: 10,000 Kronen = 1 Schilling.
1926	Richard Zsigmondy (born in Vienna in 1865) receives the Nobel prize for chemistry.
1927	Julius Wagner-Jauregg (born in Wels in the province of Upper Austria in 1857) receives the Nobel prize for his work on the malaria treatment of general paresis.
	The Austrian economy flourishes briefly; nearly 80 per cent of the money in circulation is covered by gold and foreign exchange reserves.

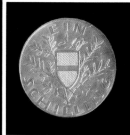

Obverse and reverse of one-Schilling coin of 1924

Ten-Schilling banknote dated 3 January, 1927

A rough sketch by Berthold Löffler

The front and back of this Jugendstil note were both designed by Berthold Löffler (born at Nieder-Rosenthal, Bohemia, in 1874, died in Vienna in 1960), décor and historical painter, graphic artist and specialist in arts and crafts. He became a professor at the Vienna College of Arts and Crafts in 1909, and a Member of the Vienna Künstlerhaus in 1921; one of his students was Oskar Kokoschka.

The front of the note carries a half-length portrait of the god Mercury, with the caduceus and a stylised lightning flash in his hands. The back shows a Danube nymph against a view of the Danube near Dürnstein in the Wachau region, with a passenger steamer of the DDSG, the Austrian Danube Steamship Company. The artist's wife Melitta (née Feldkirchner) was the model for both Mercury and the nymph.

The note was in circulation from 1927 to 1936.

Five-Schilling banknote dated 1 July, 1927

Rudolf Junk designed the note, and also drew the view of the Erzberg in Styria; the engineer with his compasses is taken from a portrait by Karl Sterrer.

The note was withdrawn in January 1936, following the issue of five-Schilling divisional coins in 1934. New five-Schilling notes printed by a simplified process were again issued after 1947, but were called in when five-Schilling coins were reintroduced in 1952.

1930	*Karl Landsteiner, doctor and immunologist (born in Vienna in 1868) receives the Nobel prize for his identification of blood types.*
1931	*Peak of the Depression in Austria (unemployment remains high throughout the 1930s).*
1933	*The 1000 mark limit of the National Socialist government of the German Reich: every German travelling to Austria is forced to pay 1000 Reichsmark (at the time, 40 per cent of tourists visiting Austria were German).*
	Erwin Schrödinger (born in Vienna in 1887) receives the Nobel prize for physics (together with the Englishman Paul Dirac).
1934	*Outbreak of civil war in February in Austria: formation of the corporate state. Dollfuss, the Federal Chancellor, is assassinated by Austrian National Socialists.*

Erwin Schrödinger

View of the Erzberg, drawn by Rudolf Junk

1000-Schilling banknote dated 2 January, 1930

This was the first banknote to carry a portrait watermark in the margin. It was designed by Fritz Zerritsch, a landscape, animal, portrait, genre and mural painter, who also designed mosaics and tapestries.

The note was issued in 1931; around 600,000 were printed, and about 15,000 were in circulation in 1933. It was withdrawn in 1938 but reissued in 1945 and 1947, in a modified and re-dated version that was printed by the two-colour offset technique. Because of the scarcity of resources after World War II, these interim banknotes were of poor quality and were widely forged.

Ten-Schilling banknote dated 2 January, 1933

The banknote's designer was Artur Brusenbauch (born in Bratislava in 1881, died in Vienna in 1957), a landscape, nude, portrait and still-life painter. This individualistic post-Impressionist joined the Vienna Sezession in 1920 and the Künstlerhaus in 1939.

The woman on the face of the banknote is dressed in traditional Upper Austrian costume with a gold bonnet, and is seen against a background of the ruins of Aggstein castle in the Danube valley, in the Wachau region. The reverse shows the Grossglockner, which became Austria's highest mountain when South Tyrol was ceded to Italy after World War I.

The note was printed on watermarked paper; part of the issue was produced on new intaglio presses which could print eighteen-note sheets.

The banknote was in circulation from 1934 to 1938, and was reissued in 1945 and 1947 in a simplified version.

Artur Brusenbauch's drawing of the Grossglockner

1936	*Otto Loewi, university professor in Vienna from 1906 to 1938, receives the Nobel prize for physiology and medicine (together with H.H. Dale).*
	Viktor Franz Hess receives the Nobel prize for physics.
1938	*German troops march into Austria in March: Austria annexed by the German Reich. The Austrian National Bank liquidated and its stock of monetary gold (more than 78,000 kg) appropriated by the German Reichsbank.*
1945	*Foundation of the Second Republic of Austria. Austria occupied by the four Allies. Wolfgang E. Pauli (born in Vienna in 1900), quantum theoretician, receives the Nobel prize for physics.*
	The National Bank Transition Act makes the continuation of the Austrian National Bank's existence possible.
	The Schilling Act: exchange of Reichsmark and Allied Military Schilling at a rate of 1:1.

1000

1027   24743   ZWEITE AUSGABE

Zehn
Schilling

Oesterreichische
Nationalbank
Wien, am 2. Jänner 1933

Präsident
Generalrat   Generaldirektor

10   10

1,000-Schilling banknote of 1930,
designed by Fritz Zerritsch: detail of front

10   Die Nachmachung der
Banknoten wird gesetz-
lich bestraft   10

A. BRUSENBAUCH INV.   J. SALBABA SCULP.

100-Schilling banknote dated 3 January, 1949

This was the first Austrian note to carry a security thread. It was designed by Erhard Amadeus-Dier (born in Vienna in 1893, died at Klosterneuburg near Vienna in 1969), portrait, landscape and still life painter as well as graphic artist, and engraved by the Viennese engraver Rupert Franke (1888–1971). Introduced in 1949, it was withdrawn ten years later.

The front carried an "ideal portrait" – a female head in profile – together with a cherub sitting on baroque scrolls and playing a double flute. The reverse shows a Danube nymph and a cherub sitting on a pedestal, with views of Vienna and St Stephen's Cathedral, the hills of the Vienna Woods and the Danube valley.

Intaglio printed detail
from the 100-Schilling note, back

20-Schilling banknote dated 2 January, 1950

This note was also designed by Erhard Amadeus-Dier and engraved by Rupert Franke. It was the first Austrian banknote to carry the portrait of a famous Austrian, that of the composer Joseph Haydn (1732–1809) at the age of 60, taken from a painting by Thomas Hardy. It circulated between 1950 and 1957.

1946	*First food deliveries to Austria by UNRRA.*
	German property seized by the Russian occupation forces.
1947	*Currency Protection Act: the nominal value of the notes in circulation reduced by two-thirds, and new banknotes authorised.*
1948	*Austria joins the International Monetary Fund. The second aid agreement (the "Marshall Plan") is concluded between Austria and the United States.*
1949	*Foundation of the Council of Europe (Austria becomes a member in 1956).*
	First use of the "LD process" in the VOEST works at Linz to smelt iron.
1950	*Food rationing in Austria ends.*
1951	*For the first time, Austrians elect a Federal President: Theodor Körner, mayor of Vienna since 1945.*

2. AUFLAGE

The Vienna Belvedere: detail from the ten-Schilling note of 1950 (back)

Eisenstadt church in the Burgenland: detail from the 20-Schilling note of 1950 (back)

JOSEPH HAYDN

100-Schilling banknote dated 1 July, 1960

The Austrian National Bank's own designer, the graphic artist Roman Hellmann (born at Schwarzach-St Veit in the Province of Salzburg in 1921), was responsible for this note, which was in circulation from 1961 to 1972.

The front of the note honours Johann Strauss the Younger, the Vienna Waltz King, and carries his portrait, together with a violin, a partly rolled-up scroll of a score and a laurel twig. The scroll shows the first bars of the "Blue Danube", Austria's unofficial national anthem. The reverse carries a view of Schönbrunn Palace, the work of the architect Johann Bernhard Fischer von Erlach and the home of the Habsburgs, and the scene of magnificent festivities during the Congress of Vienna (1814–15).

Theatre programme of the classic opera "Die Fledermaus"

1955	15 May: the Austrian State Treaty signed at the Belvedere Palace in Vienna. The National Bank Act is passed by Parliament.
	Parliament legislates for Austria's permanent neutrality. Austria joins the United Nations.
1956	Revolt in Hungary: 200,000 refugees from Hungary flee to Austria.
1957	Foundation of the International Atomic Energy Agency in Vienna.
	Constitution of the Parity Commission on Wages and Prices and the Social Partnership.
1959	Convertibility of the Schilling.
1960	Austria joins the European Free Trade Association.
1961	President Kennedy meets Khrushchev in Vienna.
	World Bank Congress in Vienna.
1962	Max Perutz (born in Vienna in 1914) receives the Nobel prize for chemistry.
1964	The IXth Winter Olympic Games held in Innsbruck.
1967	Headquarters of the United Nations Industrial Development Organization (UNIDO) opened in Vienna.
1969	The Austrian National Bank's gold reserves exceed 635,000 kg.

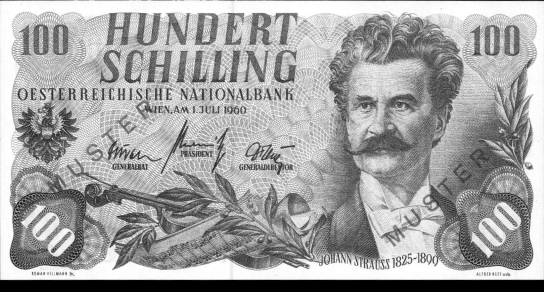

100 HUNDERT SCHILLING **100**

OESTERREICHISCHE NATIONALBANK

WIEN, AM 1. JULI 1960

GENERALRAT   PRÄSIDENT   GENERALDIREKTOR

JOHANN STRAUSS 1825-1899

ROMAN HELLMANN fec.   ALFRED NEFE sculp.

100 **100**

HUNDERT SCHILLING

100 **100**

C 878646 N

100 C 878646 N **100**

SCHLOSS SCHÖNBRUNN

ROMAN HELLMANN fec.   ALFRED NEFE sculp.

50

Fourteenth-century paper money

CHINA

Paper money is born

The earliest paper money appeared in Sichuan Province at the end of the tenth century. At the time, iron coins were used as the official currency, but iron was heavy and of low value, and it was difficult to transport sufficient weights of coins for transactions. For the sake of convenience, people deposited cash in shops in exchange for deposit bills, which carried no signature and which were transferable. These bills were an early kind of paper money.

At the beginning of the eleventh century, a group of merchants jointly issued a kind of paper money, called Jiao Zi, which could be deposited, circulated and cashed. Jiao Zi was printed from engraved plates, with a registration of black and red. Scenery and figures were engraved on the plates to deter forgers. Each merchant used an individual secret mark on the Jiao Zi that he issued, so that he could identify his own paper money when it was collected and redeemed.

Merchants transporting copper coins (a picture taken from a long painted scroll)

Because Jiao Zi was a kind of exchange bill, the more Jiao Zi issued, the more of the money supply was in the hands of the merchants. Inevitably, some merchants had their fingers in the till, with the result that eventually they failed to cash the bills on demand. Lawsuits were filed by those who had been defrauded and the government was forced to take over the right of issue of Jiao Zi.

The first government paper money was issued by the Song dynasty, in 1024. So that people would accept the new notes, they were designed to look much of the same as the old ones – a plate of the Song dynasty's first paper money, still in existence, shows this clearly.

Jiao Zi, as it appears in an ancient Chinese book

| 804 | *"Flying money" (a kind of bankers' draft) is introduced in the Tong dynasty: merchants could deposit cash in institutions in the capital city in exchange for receipts that could then be cashed elsewhere. ("Flying money" was not actually paper money, but became its predecessor.)* |
| 1024 | *Issue of paper money is taken over by the government; a special issue bureau (Jiao Zi Wu) is established to print official Jiao Zi, a kind of bill given in exchange for metal currency.* |

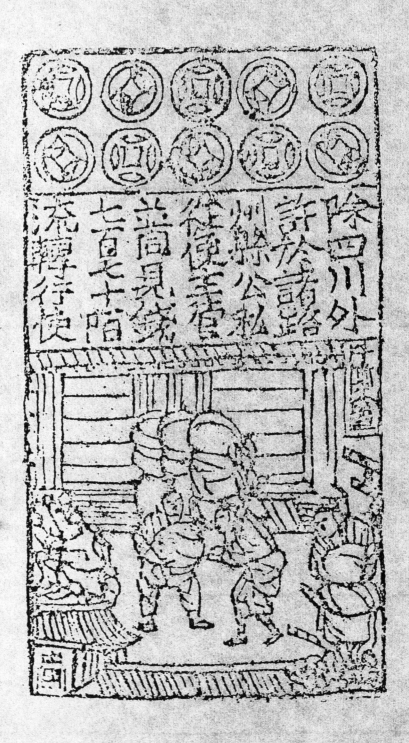

Early paper money

Engraved copper plate for printing notes

Early printing techniques

The engraved plate printing technique (similar to present-day letterpress printing) was invented at least seven centuries ago and was used mainly in book production. The merchants printed their Jiao Zi from engraved wooden plates like those used in book printing. But wooden plates were not durable, and a large quantity of paper money was required; this meant that a great many plates had to be engraved, and it was difficult to engrave all of them identically, to deter counterfeiting.

This was why, when the government took over the issue of paper money, copperplate printing techniques were introduced. An engraved master copper plate was used to cast other identical plates, to meet the increasing demand for money. This technique was also used to print the paper money of the later Jin, Yuan, Ming and Qing dynasties.

1137   *The earliest military Hui Zi, based on a silver standard, is issued by the military chief Wu Jie while guarding the border for the Song dynasty (this type of Hui Zi could be circulated only in districts where the military were stationed).*

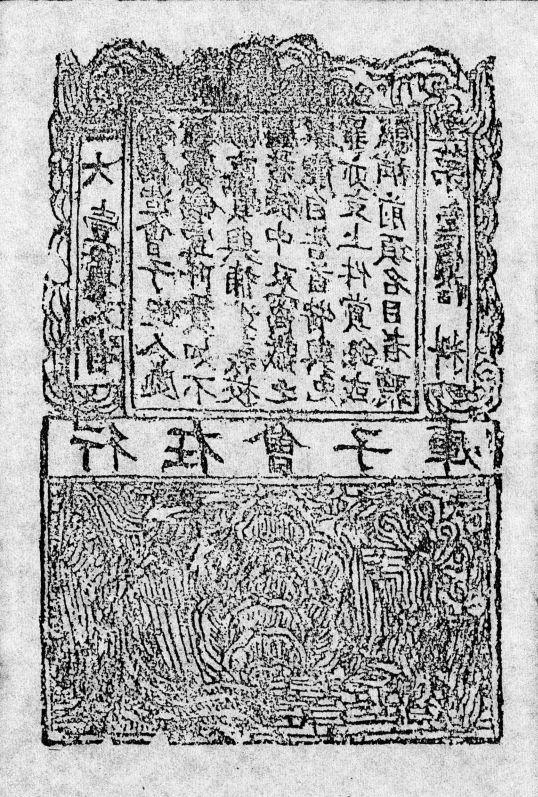

print made from the copper plate opposite

Mulberry bark paper

Bamboo

Paper was invented in China at the beginning of the Hang dynasty and was used in printing books in the Song dynasty. There were two main kinds of paper in ancient China: one made from bamboo and the other made from tree barks. Banknotes were made from the latter kind, using the inner layer of the bark of the mulberry tree, which was crushed, pulped and handmade into sheets on bamboo screens. Mulberry bark paper was thick and coarse, but stood up well to folding and rubbing. The Song government ordered paper from several districts; it also took over the paper mills in these districts and strictly prohibited private dealing.

In 1168, the Song government established the first state paper mill, Chao Huo Zhi Tu; similar mills were also set up in the Jin, Yuan and Ming dynasties. Because of its composition, the greyish-green mulberry bark paper was very difficult to forge; even so, some counterfeiters set up their own paper mills, and government regulations laid down that whenever counterfeiters were caught, all the related paper manufacturers should be arrested and severely punished.

To counter the problems a minister of the Qing dynasty suggested to the Emperor in 1853 that patterns be engraved on the bamboo papermaking screen, thus forming a watermark. But at the time the government was dealing with an economic crisis and a consequent urgent demand for money production, and the suggestion was not followed up.

| 1154 | *Paper money is issued by the Jin dynasty, a government founded by a minor nationality in northern China. (During its confrontation with the Song dynasty, the dynasty gained experience of paper money and established special banknote paper mills).* |
| 1160 | *In the Song dynasty, Hui Zi Wu is formally established and starts the issue of Xing Zai Hui Zi (a type of circulating bill that was not exchangeable for cash.* |

蕩料入簾　　　　透火焙乾

Early drawings of papermaking and drying

Remains of ancient paper money found in the desert

The numbering of ancient paper money

All early Chinese paper money was stamped with the seal of the issuing department; the notes of the Jin dynasty (1115–1234 A.D.), were stamped with the place where the paper could be redeemed as well. Every note was also numbered, not in figures but in Chinese characters. (In ancient China, there was a popular children's textbook, called *The One Thousand Character Classic*, in which 1,000 Chinese characters in daily use were selected and compiled into simple verses. By combining any two of these thousand characters, 1,000,000 notes could be uniquely numbered.)

During the Jin dynasty, an advanced letterpress printing technique was introduced. On the front of the printing plate was a hollow which could hold movable type. On the right-hand side of the plate, and integral with it, was the seal appointing the place for the redemption of the note. Using these letterpress and dead seal techniques, the notes could be numbered and stamped with the seal in a single pass.

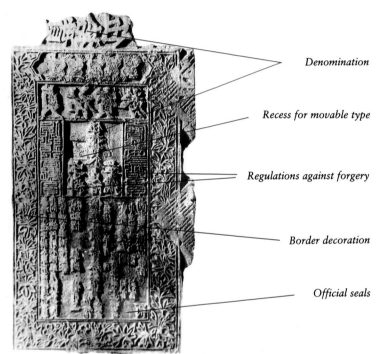

Denomination

Recess for movable type

Regulations against forgery

Border decoration

Official seals

Copper plate for printing banknotes; made during the Jin Dynasty

1207	The establishment in the Jin dynasty of the Banknote Law Treaty, the first set of regulations for the issue of paper money, although some regulations had been passed by the Song and Jin dynasties. Counterfeits are recognised as a danger, and officials in the Jin dynasty are ordered to take special care in checking for them.
1214	Paper money becomes devalued, and large-denomination notes are printed for the first time in the Jin dynasty, the highest value raised from 10 guan to 1000 guan.
1223	Currency printed on silk is used for the first time in the Jin dynasty to replace the devalued paper money (silk was used to give the public confidence, and also to deter counterfeiters).

148

The oldest paper money extant

Kublai Khan (1215–94)

Marco Polo's home city of Venice

The first news of China's use of paper money was carried to the western world by a French priest, William of Rubruk. In 1254, carrying a confidential letter from King Louis IX, he had an audience with Mangu, the grandson of the great Mongolian Ghengis Khan. When William returned to Europe, he mentioned Mangu's paper money in his report to the French king.

In 1260, Mangu was succeeded by his brother Kubla, who became the first Emperor of the Yuan dynasty. Within a year of his accession a unified paper money system, called Zhong Tong Yuan Bao Jiao Chao, was issued in northern China. In 1277 the Emperor abolished metal currency, and paper money then became the only legal circulating currency in the Yuan Empire.

Some of the copper printing plates used to print notes for the Song and Jin dynasties still survive, but the earliest paper money known to exist today is that of the Yuan dynasty. The notes were printed by a complicated process, after which they were worked on by hand before they were issued. The back carried patterns symbolising the denomination, and both sides were stamped with the red seals of the three controlling departments and a black seal across the seam on the upper left-hand side. These measures showed the importance of the issue and also helped to deter forgers.

At the end of the thirteenth century, when the Venetian traveller Marco Polo introduced paper money to the west, he reported that the Great Khan controlled much more wealth than any other emperor in the world – through the issue of paper money.

1227	*The army of Genghis Khan issues silk-based money in Shandong Province.*
1255	*A French priest, William of Rubruk, brings reports of the Mongolian paper money to the west.*
1260	*The Emperor Kubla of the Yuan dynasty issues Zhong Tong Yuan Bao Jiao Chao.*
1277	*Kubla stops the circulation of metal currency throughout the country, which now becomes the first in the world to use paper money only.*

Early banknotes and auxiliary currency

The early notes carried handwritten values, but after the eleventh century the government issued notes of different denominations. As the paper money was based on copper cash, the denominations were the same as for the coins: for example, the wen and kuan (1 kuan = 100 wen).

On the Zhong Tong Yuan Bao Jiao Chao, issued in 1260 by the Yuan dynasty, the number of denominations was increased: one- and two-kuan and 10- and 100-wen notes were now available. In 1351, the system of currency based on metal coinage was changed to a new one based on paper money. At the same time, copper coins were struck for use as auxiliary currency, and denominations of one, two, five, ten and 25 wen were issued.

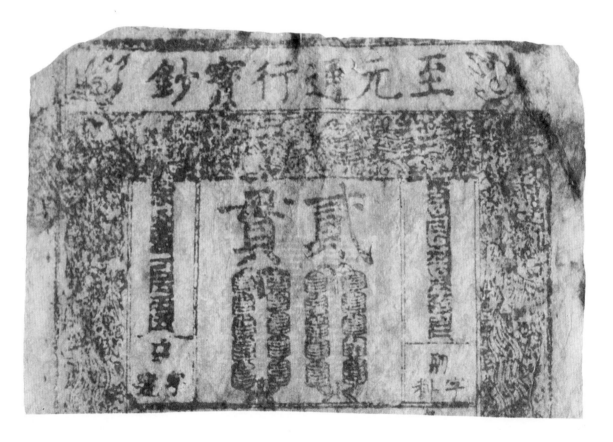

| 1350 | *The Yuan dynasty carries out reforms to the currency system; old notes are stamped with seals before use as new notes. The new notes become the basic currency, and copper coins of smaller values are also issued.* |

152

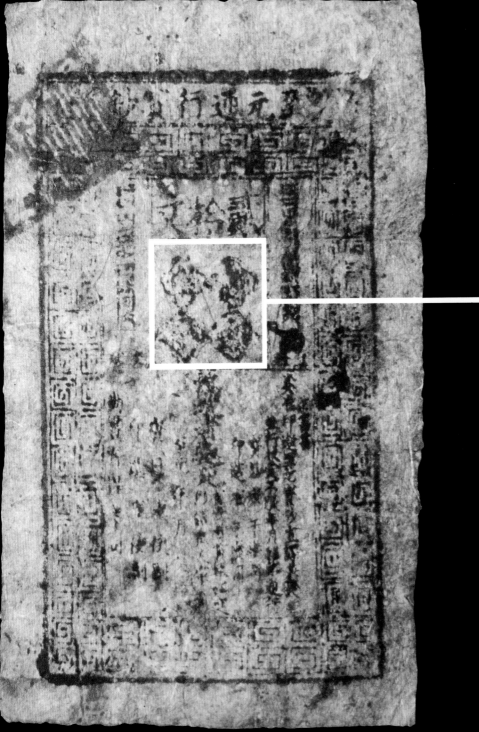

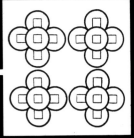

Patterns symbolising the denomination of a bank note

Fourteenth-century copper coins

Early banknote designs

The Chinese authorities understood that banknotes decorated with vignettes and patterns were not only attractive but also (and more importantly) offered some protection against forgery.

A thirteenth-century hand engraved printing plate for making forged banknotes

Most of the early Chinese banknotes carried illustrations of houses, trees and figures. In the middle of the twelfth century the banknotes of the Jin dynasty introduced ornamental borders and, prominently displayed, the laws and regulations providing for the beheading of counterfeiters and the rewarding of those who informed on them, together with the signatures of the printers and the issuers. This style was followed by generations of later Chinese notes, of which the beautiful design of the fourteenth-century notes of Da Ming Tong Xing Bao Chao of the Ming dynasty is typical: the sharp scales of the dragon symbolising royal power can be clearly seen in the illustration opposite.

Of course, people tried to counterfeit the new notes, using soft low-melting metals to cast flat plates onto which designs were engraved by hand; work of this kind is fairly common in old Chinese books. The quality of the home-made plates was far below that of the genuine ones, however; the difference can still be seen in surviving specimens.

1375	The newly founded Ming Empire issues Da Ming Tong Xing Bao Chao for circulation with the copper coins. (As a mark of respect to the First Emperor of the New Empire, the title on the paper money issued by his descendants was not changed. The Da Ming Tong Xing Bao Chao circulated for more than a century, and was withdrawn only because of its devaluation).
1643	Army mutinies in the Ming dynasty. The Government tries to meet the crisis by preparing an issue of new paper money, but fails.
1853	Army mutinies in the south lead to a financial crisis. Two kinds of paper money are issued: one based on silver, the other on copper. (This was the last to be issued by the Central Government.)

The People's Republic's first banknotes

Banknote issued by the Central Bank of Zhonghua Soviet in 1932

China started to use modern banknote-printing techniques at the end of the last century. For several decades, however, Chinese techniques fell behind those of foreign printers, whose help had to be requested from time to time.

The People's Government issued its first series of banknotes during the war that led to the founding of the People's Republic of China. It was essentially a wartime currency, and design, platemaking and printing were carried out piecemeal. The series included ten denominations but sixty different notes, with different sizes, colours and designs for the same denomination. All sorts of improvised facilities and materials were used to produce them, depending on the war situation: the designs were put together from part-designs of other notes available at the time, and they were printed partly by letterpress, partly by offset and partly by rotary-plate presses on both imported banknote-quality material and ordinary wood-free paper. But in spite of its fragmented and extempore production, this series of Ren Min Bi were an important feature of the birth of the People's Republic.

1908	*The first professional banknote printing plant is established by the Bureau of Printing under Du Zhi Bu (the Ministry of Finance) of the Qing government in Beijing.*
1910	*The first set of steel intaglio plates for printing the Da Qing Bank's exchange bills is manufactured by the Bureau of Printing.*
1932	*The first central bank (Central Bank of Zhonghua Soviet) set up by the revolutionary government of the Communist Party of China issues paper money.*
1948	*The People's Bank of China is formally established. Issue of the first series of Ren Min Bi – the banknote of the People's Republic – begins.*

The engraver's art in China

The foundation of the People's Republic of China changed the whole position. The need for a unified series of banknotes became pressing, while at the same time the development of the economy had created the right conditions for improving printing techniques. The second, third and fourth series of Ren Min Bi, issued from 1955 onwards, incorporated improved registration of intaglio and offset printing, while the engravers who prepared the intaglio plates reached standards of excellence hitherto unknown.

The two-yuan note of the second series of Ren Min Bi shows the pagoda at Yanan. Yanan stands on the Loess Plateau, the cradle of the Chinese nation; it was in Yanan that the Central Committee of the Chinese Communist Party lived during World War II. The rugged landscape is criss-crossed by steep-sided gullies carved out of the hillsides by long years of wind and rain. The engravers have used the terrain's pattern of strongly marked curves as a setting for the straight, clean lines of the pagoda on the hilltop, which thus stands out as a powerful symbol of the reverence in which Yanan is held in the heart of the Chinese people.

The main scene on the reverse of the one-yuan note of the third series of Ren Min Bi, "Grazing on Tien Shan", was engraved in several different styles. The engravers used heavy straight lines for the thick forest, short lines and dots for the mountain ranges and formalised curves for the flock of sheep. The whole picture is richly constructed, with a strong perspective.

The combinations of hand- and machine-engraved patterns not only make up fine works of art but also, due to the variety of the engraving techniques, are very effective anti-counterfeiting features.

"The Steelworker", engraved by Wu Pengyue

1951	*The designs of the second series of Ren Min Bi are produced; platemaking, trial printing and production begin.*
1955	*The issue of the second series of Ren Min Bi begins, with old notes being exchanged at a rate of one to 10,000.*

"The Pagoda Mountain in Yanan", engraved by Wu Pengyue

"Grazing in Tien Shan", engraved by Ju Wenjun

Tien An Men watermark, designed by Zheng Xinchen

Watermarking

The watermark of a banknote – easily seen by the user, and difficult to imitate – is a useful protection against forgery. Chinese banknote manufacturers had planned to introduce watermarked notes as early as the mid-nineteenth century, but they were not actually produced until 1960, after the founding of the People's Republic of China.

A start was made by using a simple pattern of five stars – a pattern once carried by ancient coins – on full-page watermarked paper. During the development trials, both the manufacturing technology and the papermarking materials were improved, giving the notes better resistance to creasing and a clearer watermark.

Although this marked a considerable advance, the full-page watermarked paper could not meet the standard of counterfeit-deterrence needed for high denomination notes. Further improvements were introduced, and engineers, engravers and printers co-operated to produce the first fixed-watermarked banknote paper ("Tien An Men" paper), used to print ten-yuan Ren Min Bi in 1963.

The paper used for the fourth series of Ren Min Bi, issued in 1987, is of a still higher grade. The fixed portrait watermarks used on the ten-, 50- and 100-yuan notes are technically more complicated than the older five star and Tien An Men watermarks, which were formed by geometric lines, and of far higher quality, thanks to the attention paid by the technicians to improving the watermark through the whole process of designing, engraving, mouldmaking and papermaking.

1959	*Paper watermarked with a five-star pattern is developed.*
1960	*Banknote paper with the fixed Tian An Men watermark is developed.*
1961	*A four colour dry offset/Orloff printing press is built in China, and awarded the National Invention Prize.*

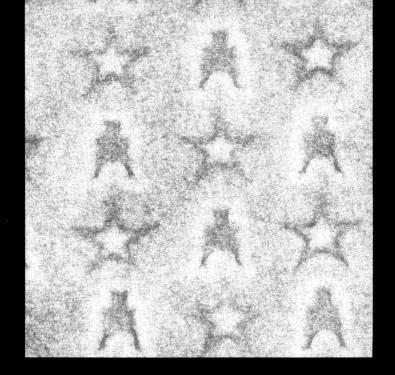

Portraits of a worker and of Chairman Mao, by Hu Fuging:
watermarks used on the fourth series of Ren Min Bi

The dry offset/Orloff multicolour technique

The issue of the third series of Ren Min Bi, the first series of banknotes to be printed entirely in China, began in 1964. The series introduced new design styles, with richer and more varied colours; demands on the ink were much higher and the printing more difficult.

The Chinese authorities found, however, that banknotes printed on ordinary commercial presses were fairly easy to counterfeit, while those produced by specially imported banknote-printing presses were of poor quality. After reviewing all the equipment available they decided to introduce the technique of dry offset/Orloff multicolour printing, which uses the principle of indirect transfer printing. In this process different inks from several printing plates are first collected and then transferred to one plate and printed onto the paper; in a variant of the method, inks of different colours are collected onto different parts of a rubber cylinder and then transferred to the printing plate. The technique gives accurate registration, and allows the designer to introduce complicated colour schemes, rich tones and even lines of several different colours. The two sides of the notes can be produced in one pass, giving a high-quality finished product that is extremely difficult to counterfeit.

| 1962 | *A multicolour simultaneous printing press is built, and awarded the National Scientific Invention Prize.* |
| 1963 | *Four-colour intaglio printing is invented in China.* |

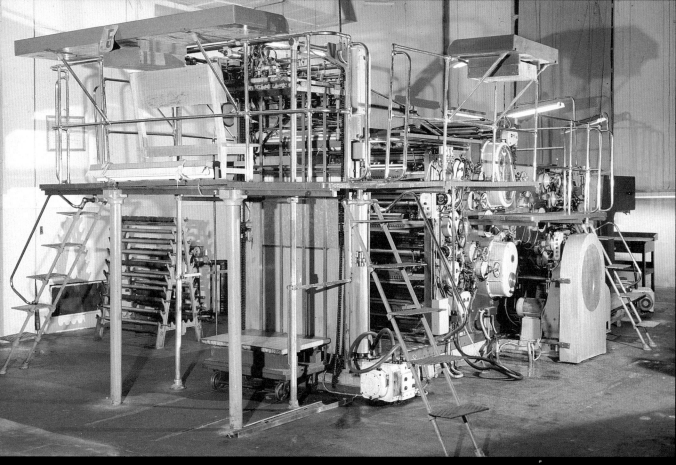

Dry offset multicolour press,
designed by engineers Zhu Huanmin, Li Genxu, Chen Hongge, Mi Wangdou

Orloff print (detail from the ten-yuan note of 1965)

Co-ordinated designs

The first series of Ren Min Bi were designed and printed in piecemeal fashion during the war that led to the founding of the Republic, and their illustrations of figures, landscapes, ships and factories represented a somewhat *ad hoc* approach. On the other hand, the second series of Ren Min Bi, were linked by a single theme created through the co-operation between famous artists, including Luo Gongliu, Zhou Lingzhao and Hou Yimin, and the printers' technical staff. This theme was the founding of a new China by the people: the three-, two- and one-yuan notes showed the monuments of Jing Gang Mountain, Yanan and Tien An Men respectively, representing different periods of the Chinese revolution, while the five- and ten-yuan notes showed parades of workers and peasants, symbolising the New China, of which the people had become the masters.

The designs of the fourth series of Ren Min Bi are even more closely linked. The main motif on the 100-yuan note shows the four founders of New China, and on the five-yuan note are portraits of peasants and both blue-collar and white-collar workers, who make up the mass of the Chinese people. On each of the notes from ten yuan to one jiao are two portraits of different Chinese nationalities. The whole series pursues the theme of the united effort of all the Chinese nationalities in the building of the China of today.

中國人民銀行

叁圓　　　叁圓

3　　　3

一九五三年

I II III 0000000　　　I II III 0000000

貳圓　　　2

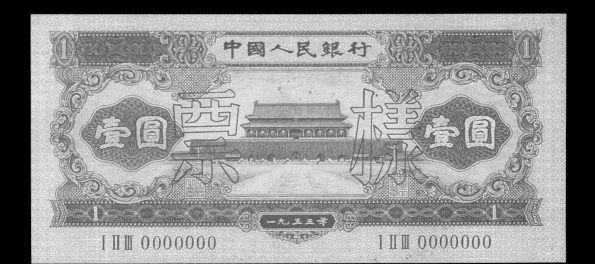

中國人民銀行

壹圓　　　壹圓

1　　　1

一九五三年

I II III 0000000　　　I II III 0000000

The national style of decoration

The borders and decorations on banknotes often display the national style of the issuing country, and those of the second series of Ren Min Bi are no exception.

The artists of ancient China had used the shapes and patterns of plants and floating clouds on porcelain, embroidery and furniture, and even on buildings! The designers of the second series of Ren Min Bi daringly broke the traditional frame structure and decorated their notes with the same patterns, such as the exquisite floating clouds on the back of the two-yuan note.

The national style on the fourth series of Ren Min Bi is even more strongly marked, using many patterns drawn from the woven textiles of the various ethnic groups of China. The patterns in the background on the back of the 50-yuan note are derived from the designs on Shang dynasty bronzes more than three thousand years old; they are combined with a view of the mother river of the Chinese nation (the Yellow River), to convey not only a strong national flavour but also a profound sense of history.

*Shang Dynasty bronze trough
(3,000 years old)*

166

中国人民銀行
貳圓

1953

00037

ZHONGGUO RENMIN YINHANG

50

WU SHI YUAN

50

1980

Cunguo Yinzmin Yinzhang hasdibmanz

A new standard of excellence

The fourth series of Ren Min Bi, with its portraits of China's national leaders and ordinary people, gave Chinese craftsmen the chance to show what they could do. The modelling of the facial features, and the textures of thick hair and beards, of ethnic costume and jewellery, were translated by the engravers into intaglio plates of superb quality. To the traditional decorations of the notes were added vignettes of swallows, phoenix, pine and bamboo – all symbolising luck and happiness – and on the fronts of the one- to ten-yuan notes these were used as the backgrounds for the lettering. The designs are rich in both line and colour, to exploit the full capabilities of the new Orloff presses. In the way in which the new series has married machine and hand engraving of the plates, in its bringing together of offset, intaglio, rainbow and Orloff printing techniques, and in its use of complex watermarking to deter counterfeiting, it represents the peak of modern China's banknote-production technology.

Two-yuan Ren Men Bi, with portraits of Uigur and Yi girls engraved by Yu Yongcai

| 1964 | Issue of third series of Ren Min Bi begins; all old notes are redeemed on a one-to-one basis. (Since then, all Ren Min Bi have been produced entirely in China.) |
| 1987 | Issue of fourth series of Ren Min Bi begins, using fixed-portrait watermarked paper; the notes circulate together with the third series. |

Five-yuan Ren Men Bi, with portraits of a Tibetan woman and an elderly Hui man engraved by Li Bin

100-yuan Ren Men Bi, with relief portraits of the Four Leaders engraved by Su Xihua

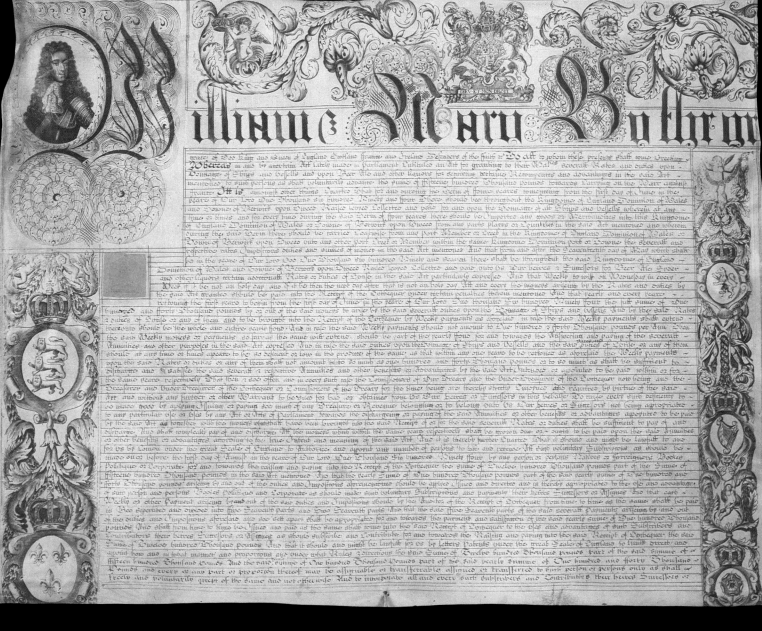

Detail from the Bank of England Charter of 1694

The first Britannia to be used on an issued note

ENGLAND

"Rags make paper
Paper makes money
Money makes banks
Banks make loans
Loans make beggars
Beggars make rags . . ."

For thousands of years, people put their trust in precious metals, particularly gold and silver. Today they accept paper money just as confidently.

English paper money originated in the handwritten receipts given by goldsmiths in exchange for cash deposits. In 1694 the Bank of England adopted these goldsmiths' "notes" as the basis of its own, and under the powerful forces of legislation, technological innovation and social and economic change, these simple documents have evolved into today's sophisticated banknotes.

The Bank's first notes

The "Glorious Revolution" of 1688 brought to Britain a new political, religious and economic freedom, the foundation of the country's rise to commercial and military pre-eminence in eighteenth-century Europe. All kinds of novel concepts came to fruition in the climate of this newfound freedom, one of which had been debated on and off for some forty years and finally came to transform the course of the economic development of Britain: the concept of the Bank of England.

The successful proposal for the new national bank came from a London-based Scots entrepreneur, William Paterson. His first idea, put forward in 1691, had been rejected by the parliamentary committee – perhaps partly, as he later wrote, because "others said this project came from Holland and therefore would not hear of it, since we had too many Dutch things", but certainly also because he and his backers required that, in return for a loan of £1,000,000, the bills they issued should be made legal tender. The scheme foundered; within two or three years, however, Paterson tried again, and his new plan for a "Bank of England" omitted any mention of bills. The

revised plan was accepted by Parliament, and the Bank of England Act 1694 was passed – some six years after William of Orange came to the English throne. Neither Paterson's revised proposal nor the Bank's Royal Charter mentioned banknotes, but Paterson and his friends were clearly wide awake to the profitability of issuing notes and meant to do so as soon as the Bank had been established; indeed, within hours of the Charter's being sealed the Directors of the Bank were discussing how to go about it.

London um 1665

1665	*The Great Plague reaches London.*
1666	*The Great Fire of London.*
	Newton's discovery of the law of gravitation.
	Milton writes Paradise Lost.
1667	*First part of John Bunyan's* Pilgrim's Progress *is published.*
1677	*Marriage of William of Orange to Mary Stuart.*
1679	*Habeas Corpus Act passed.*
1688	*The "Glorious Revolution".*
1694	*Bank of England founded.*

William of Orange

172

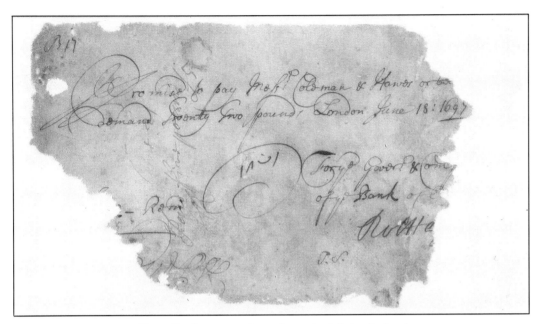

The earliest known running cash note (entirely handwritten)

The Court of Directors met for the first time on the afternoon of Friday 27 July 1694, a few hours after the Charter's sealing. They decided that depositors would be permitted to choose one of three methods for having their deposits of cash – that is to say, coin – acknowledged; all three were already practised by the goldsmith-bankers. Of these three methods one – the running cash note – was the most direct antecedent of modern notes. The note was issued for the full amount of the deposit and was endorsed by the Bank cashier as and when part of the sum was encashed, and was made payable to the depositor or "bearer", an option which allowed such notes to circulate. The text was printed in a cursive script reminiscent of the handwritten goldsmiths' notes. Over the next few decades three security devices were introduced: a medallion of Britannia, based on the Bank's corporate seal; distinctive watermarked paper; and the "sum block", which showed a pound sign followed by the amount.

It was a form that London citizens would find familiar, and therefore acceptable. The act of accepting a note is a wordless assertion of faith in the issuer's promise to pay. The notes were in fact promissory notes, because the Bank undertook to pay – or perhaps more accurately repay – the amount of the deposit whenever requested to do so. These promissory notes carried all the elements

Britannia as she appeared on the £50 note of 1760

An eighteenth-century sum block

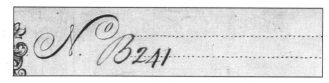

The number and signature clause on a £50 note of 1760

of today's Bank notes. They carried a number that indicated where in the Bank's books that particular liability was recorded; they showed, of course, the amount of the deposit and this later developed into denominations which allowed them to circulate yet more easily. They were signed by the cashier who received the deposit "For the Governor and Company of the Bank of England"; these familiar words are still used today.

The Bank's directorate decided that the new corporation's common seal should represent "Britannia sitting and looking at a bank of money" – probably Britannia was chosen because she had appeared on halfpennies and farthings for more than twenty years. She appeared on all printed notes, as indeed, she still does, although details

of the Britannia design are constantly changing, under the influence of the fashions, tastes, styles and even technology of the day. But the Bank's Britannia of today, now the Bank's badge, differs from her counterpart at the Royal Mint in that she is most definitely land-based. She is sitting, carries a spear and looks on the bank of money, and at her side there is a cross of St George, the Mint's Britannia of today, on the other hand, has clear nautical attributes: being helmeted, with the sea in the background, and carrying the trident (a three-pointed spear of Poseidon or Neptune, the god of the sea. There is even a theory that Britannia might be the origin of the Bank's nickname, the Old Lady, but there is no evidence to support it. The source of the nickname might perhaps have been an inexpert engraving in which she looked a little too elderly for the personification of the recently founded Bank.

1694 halfpenny coin with the design that inspired the Bank's Britannia

Four days after the Bank opened for business the Directors decided that running cash notes should be printed, but these printed notes were almost certainly never issued. The minutes of the Court of Directors record that "the notes for running cash being considered liable to be counterfeited, for preventing thereof it was ordered that they be done on marbled paper indented". Meanwhile notes were entirely handwritten. Eventually new printed notes appeared, but no sooner were they issued than a forgery was discovered. Once again all running cash notes had to be handwritten but this sparked off an investigation into the feasibility of using paper with a special watermark. This key security measure was eventually introduced into the Bank's notes in 1697: it had a looped border with a scroll on the left and a panel bearing the words "Bank of England" at the bottom.

1720	The "South Sea Bubble".
1721	Robert Walpole becomes the first British Prime Minister.
1723	Death of Sir Christopher Wren.
1726	Publication of Jonathan Swift's Gulliver's Travels.

„Wren's Cathedral"

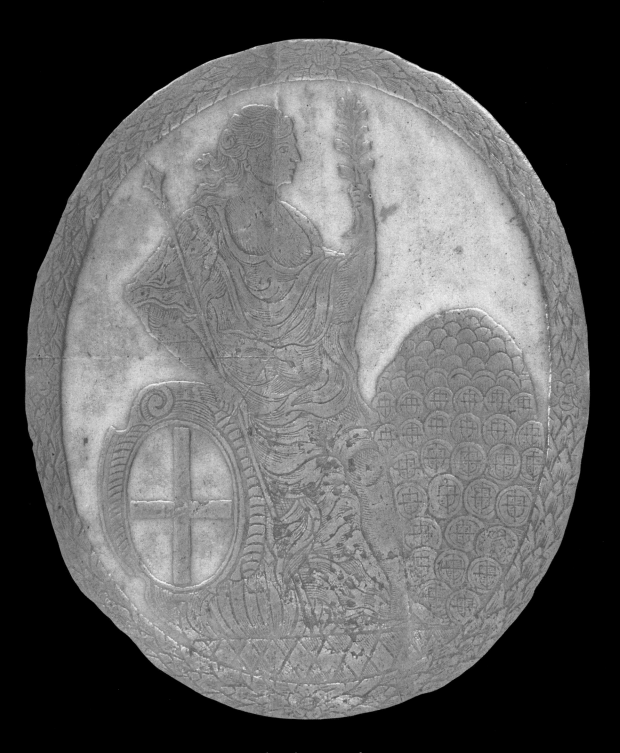

The Bank's Britannia of 1694

Although printing methods hardly altered in the eighteenth century, banknote paper continued to improve. Until then the Bank had been using a spongy, brown paper; a condemned forger in Newgate prison told a Bank cashier that if it were harder and whiter his own crime of erasing the amount with chemicals would be impossible, and in 1724, the Bank commissioned Henri Portal a Huguenot refugee, to supply "paper for banknotes of the like goodness or fitter for their service than the paper now used". Portals still provide the paper for English banknotes today.

The Bank of England

The new paper was used for the first "denominationalised" notes, printed in 1725. These notes, still only partially printed, were for round amounts, but they could be written up on issue to the sum required by the customer. The next step towards the true denominational note followed naturally. In 1743 the "sum block", an elaborate pound sign followed by the amount in white gothic letters on a black background, was introduced into the design, partly as a unique identification mark but more importantly as an anti-forgery device (Britannia similarly was used first as an identification symbol and later on as a security device). The black bead-like projections to the border of the background of the sum block gradually became more clearly defined until each denomination had its individual pattern.

The Bank of England note thus began its life as a partially printed promissory note that was filled in by the Bank's cashier with the details of the transaction and handed to the customer in exchange for a cash deposit. Gradually these pieces of paper became more widely accepted and began to represent units of value rather than specific amounts. Forgery was rife, however, and although in time the need to keep one step ahead of the forger came to stimulate improvements in note production and design, the Bank's directors at first emphasised deterrence by the gallows more than prevention by technical innovation. They held firmly that banknote security lay in the use of good-quality watermarked paper printed with a simple easily recognisable design, believing that a forgery of a simple note was harder to pass than a forgery of an intricate design which might confuse people by its very complexity. Moreover, although paper was advancing technologically, printing was not. And the Bank was printing from engraved plates until the issue of the first wholly surface printed, or letterpress, note in 1855.

1733	John Kay invents the "flying shuttle", the first of the great textile inventions.
	Jethro Tull publishes Horse-Hoeing Husbandry, *advocating new agricultural methods.*
1753	British Museum begun by Government purchase of Sloane's collection.
1764	James Hargreaves invents the "spinning Jenny".
1768	Royal Academy of Arts founded.
1769	James Watt discovers the power of steam.
	Richard Arkwright invents the water-powered spinning frame.

The "Spinning Jenny"

176

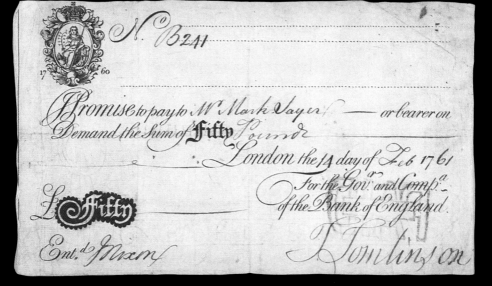

The £50 note of 1760

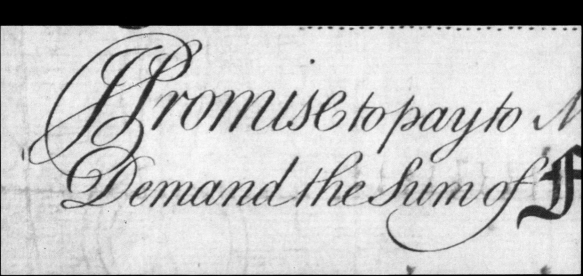

The promissory clause (enlarged)

The "Restriction" Period

The year 1797 saw the beginnings of a crisis for the Bank of England. The threat of an invasion by the army of revolutionary France a few months earlier had caused some hoarding of gold by the public but the turning point came in February, when a small group of Frenchmen under an Irish-American adventurer landed in Wales. The invaders were soon rounded up but the damage had been done; public confidence had been shaken. Prime Minister Pitt immediately acted to protect the Bank's reserves against panic withdrawals and ordered it, via the Privy Council, to stop paying cash for its notes until Parliament had considered the matter. This emergency period, christened the "Restriction Period" or the "Restriction of Cash Payments", was extended again and again, and did not end until 1821.

In time of crisis the public wants gold, not paper, and people clung to what coins they had. At that time the lowest-denomination Bank of England note was for £5, and in order to keep the wheels of commerce turning the Bank issued notes for £1 and £2. Unfortunately they did not foresee what was to happen to these lower denomination notes. They were handled by people who were largely illiterate and completely unused to paper money: they knew gold and silver and could easily tell whether a coin was counterfeit, but notes were different. Many ordinary people consequently became the natural dupes of forgers. To make matters worse, the new hastily prepared notes were a poor piece of work; they were the same size as other denominations, and their layout and style followed the same pattern. A slight improvement was made in 1798 with the introduction of a new, clearer and slightly distinctive design, in which the printed area was reduced and enclosed by a line and the deomination appeared in words at the centre top; this, however was a short-lived issue.

Bank Restriction Notice, 1797

1771	*Birth of Sir Walter Scott.*
1776	*Adam Smith's* Wealth of Nations *is published.*
1779	*Samual Crompton invents the "Spinning Mule".*
1783	*Britain recognises American independence.*
1793	*France declares war on England.*
1797	*Inconvertibility of Bank of England notes ("Restriction Period") to protect gold reserves.*

The "Spinning Mule"

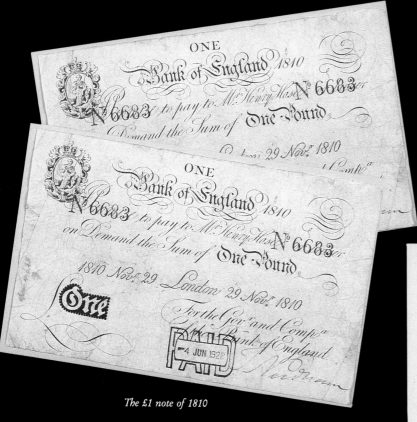

The £1 note of 1810

POLITICAL-RAVISHMENT, or The Old Lady of Threadneedle-Street in danger!

"The Old Lady of Threadneedle Street in Danger" — a cartoon by
James Gillray published in 1797. The Bank appears as an old lady
dressed in the newly issued £1 and £2 notes, who is being attacked
by Prime Minister Pitt. Pitt ignores the paper money and
goes for the gold in her pocket and treasure chest

MIDAS, Transmuting all into GOLD PAPER.

"Midas, transmuting all into paper" — Pitt is portrayed as Midas,
sucking in all the gold and emitting £1 and £2 notes

Forgery had been a hanging offence since 1697 (and it remained so until 1832) but the threat of the rope did not stop the wholesale production and uttering of forged notes during the Restriction Period. About 600 people were condemned for this crime, and over half of these were hanged; the rest were transported, mainly to the newly discovered Australia. Public outrage at the executions was intensified by anger at the Bank's apparent apathetic attitude to producing a note that was less easily forged, and the search for an "inimitable" note began. The Bank invited suggestions as to how its notes might be made more forgery-proof and over the next twenty-five years nearly 400 proposals were received. Many were impractical, such as incorporating a number in the watermark; a very few were ahead of their time, such as portraying the monarch on notes and even microprinting and printing the backs of notes by lithography. The acid test of each of these suggested improvements was for the Bank's engraver to try to copy it; inevitably, he was always successful, proving the maxim – if indeed it needed proving – that what one man can do another can copy. A novel proposal was that silk thread should be embodied in the substance of the paper (many years later this was adopted by several foreign countries as a security measure) and in 1803 the papermaker to the Banque de France, Monsieur Guillot, submitted specimens of his product. Two years earlier, however, the Bank had adopted a new watermark consisting of a distinctive waved line, and this seemed to provide adequate protection already.

Detail from 1810 £5 note, showing the waved-line watermark

In 1801 the design changes of 1798 were abandoned and the whole area of the paper was used again for the design. Other features were tried: the denomination of the £1 note was printed in italic and that of the £2 note in gothic script; in 1805, a vertical line was printed across the £2 note – it may have assisted the illiterate in identification but it was really put there to act as a guide when the note was cut in half and sent by two different posts to provide security in transit.

After a century of piecemeal development, the notes were criticised mainly on two counts: the poor technology of the printing and the conservative design of the note itself. One critic described them as being "of inferior workmanship" and said they "could be forged by anyone who can use a camel's hair pencil". Another saw their artistic content as deplorable; he wrote "I think public bodies should have some regard for the credit of their country. I understand that English art is not much respected on the continent. I hope foreigners do not take the Bank note for a specimen of English art."

1799	*Income tax imposed by Pitt the Younger.*
1805	*Battle of Trafalgar: death of Admiral Lord Nelson.*
1807	*Slave trade abolished in the British Empire.*
1815	*Battle of Waterloo, 18 June.*
1821	*Bank Restriction Period ends.*
1825	*Opening of the first steam-hauled public railway in England – Stockton to Darlington.*

Early railway engine

Cruikshank's "Bank Restriction Note" of 1818
("Jack Ketch" was the nickname given to
the public hangman)

A cartoon by S. W. Fores, published in 1818:
a suspected forger has been brought to the
Bank, but the officials cannot decide whether
his note forged or not

The Bramah numbering press installed in 1809

Every one of the Bank's notes was still dated and numbered by hand: a tedious business for the clerks. The day of their liberation dawned with the invention of a hand-operated machine that could number and date 2,000 notes per day by surface printing, (as against the maximum of 400 that a clerk with pen and ink would manage). So, in 1809, the Bank's notes began to be overprinted with the number in two places; the date also appeared twice with the word "London" in between. The use of two printing techniques – the main body of the note in intaglio and the number and date in letterpress was an effective anti-forgery device, because it meant that forgers must either cast their own type to use in conjunction with their plates, or take the risk of engraving the plates with a single number and date that would quickly become known.

Numbering on a note issued in 1810

Even so, apart from the new waved-line watermark, English notes at the end of the Restriction Period remained an invitation to forgers. The special committee set up by the Bank to look into the improvement of note security had failed to solve the problem, and two parliamentary enquiries had been equally unsuccessful. Of all the suggestions put forward, only one found any favour with the Bank: the proposal of Augustus Applegath and his partner Edward Cowper that the back of a note should bear a perfect mirror image of the front. The Bank saw their concept as coming close to the "inimitable" note. It invested money and resources in the project and provided secure accommodation, with even a steam engine to drive the machinery, and its papermakers, Portals installed special equipment on which to make paper to Applegath's specification. Single-colour printing was used in the early trials, but the later ones used as many as five colours.

But when the Restriction Period ended in May 1821, and with it the issue of £1 and £2 notes, the pressure on the Bank to solve the forgery problem faded. Moreover, even the partners' use of colour failed to prevent the Bank's engraver, William Bawtree, from copying their latest proof. The experiment was abandoned.

Two goals remained, however; to choose a design so distinctive that even if it was copied people would at once notice the difference, and to use methods of production which would make forgery expensive and difficult.

1829	Commissioner and Assistant Commissioner of Police appointed and located at Scotland Yard.
1832	Capital punishment for forgery and counterfeiting abolished.
	Electric telegraph invented by Morse.

Electric telegraph

182

The famous "white fiver", issued from 1793 until the late 1950s

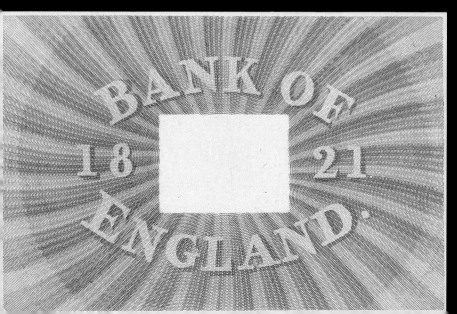

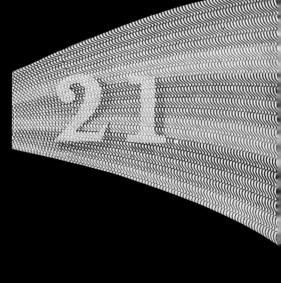

A machine-ruled design by William Bawtree, the Bank's Engraver

New methods

Detail from the only known surviving note from the Bank's Exeter Branch, which operated from 1827 to 1834

In 1825, £1 notes appeared again. A speculative boom led to country banks over-extending themselves; inevitably, the day came when a provincial bank refused to pay one of its notes in gold. Gold reserves were low, and so in order to restore public confidence and credit and protect its reserves, the Bank of England issued around a million £1 notes that had been printed during the Restriction Period but never issued. They soon reached the provinces and were accepted by the public who had previously been faithful to coin. Forgery rocketed, and in 1826 an Act was passed prohibiting any bank issuing a note for less than £5 and allowing note-issuing joint stock banks only outside a 65 mile radius of London.

The Bank's Deputy Governor returned from a visit to the Bank of Ireland in 1832 full of praise for Irish printing

methods: as a result a deputation was sent to Dublin to examine their plant. The report they submitted showed that Irish technology was well in advance of the Bank's, especially in two aspects: the method of numbering the notes (which is almost the same as that used today) and the use of a plate transfer press to prepare copy plates from a master engraving – a technique that would allow the Bank to achieve its long-term goal of the "identity", or sameness, of notes. The master engraving was done on steel, and from this other plates were rolled in soft steel and then hardened by heat treatment – that is, all the copy plates were derived direct from the master. This idea had been put forward by an American, Jacob Perkins, during the Bank's earlier search for inimitability, but the hardening of the copy plates had presented problems: the heating process often produced blemishes on the plates. But the Bank of Ireland seemed to have solved this problem and so the Bank of England took a leaf out of their book and adopted the process in 1836.

Now that printing technology was available it seemed that, given a design that combined different methods of engraving, the Bank could surely produce an unforgeable note. A committee consisting of the Bank's Governor, Deputy Governor and four of its Directors sought advice from a distinguished painter, a first-rate line engraver and the Royal Mint's designer, and eventually proposed a note that incorporated five methods of engraving; it was an extravagant, radical design, completely different from anything the Bank had produced before. The Court of Directors did not like it, however – one Director dismissed it as "a picture with a note in the middle".

1834	*"Tolpuddle Martyrs" victimised to discourage the British working class.*
1836	*Act for registration of births, deaths and marriages passed.*
1838	*National Gallery opened.*
	Death penalty abolished other than for murder or attempted murder.
1840	*Penny Post established.*
1844	*Bank Charter Act passed, aiming to give Bank of England a monopoly in the issue of English notes. The issue of notes is kept entirely separate from the Bank's commercial business.*
1847	*British Museum opened.*
	W. M. Thackeray's Vanity Fair *published.*

Penny Post

The committee-designed note of 1838

*1838 £5 note, printed using a plate transfer press, automatic numbering and steam
for warming the plates and drying the notes*

The "Five Pound Bank Note Office" in the Bank of England in 1845

Meanwhile, the Bank of England's monopoly of note issue developed further; when its Charter was renewed in 1833 joint-stock companies in London, though able to act as banks, were no longer allowed to issue notes. In 1844, the Bank Charter Act laid down that only banks already issuing notes could continue to do so and the number of notes each could circulate was regulated. When banks amalgamated, the bank that was absorbed lost its note circulation unless the new partnership had six persons or less. In the Bank of England the issue of notes was now kept entirely separate from commercial business.

In January 1855 a new design of Bank of England note came on the scene: perhaps unsurprisingly, *The Times* wrote that, "its appearance at a hasty glance is very little different from the old Note". But much care and thought had gone into the preparation of this new note, and it incorporated several important security features.

The arts were catered for with a new rendition of Britannia, this time by a Royal Academician, Daniel Maclise (incidentally, this Britannia was used on the Bank's notes for more than 100 years). The new issue was surface printed instead of using the hitherto familiar intaglio; furthermore, the printing was carried out using electrotypes which gave the elusive "identity" or sameness to the notes. It carried a new kind of watermark – it was shaded – more than forty years after the French firm of Johannot of Annonay had managed to produce such a watermark, and a dozen years after a French company had submitted a proposal for a new Bank of England note on "*papière filigrane inimitable*", which also carried a shaded watermark. The Bank had taken no notice of it at the time, however, nor did the Bank of Austria to whom specimens were also sent.

1851	*Great Exhibition in London.*
1855	*Army hospital reforms under Florence Nightingale.*
1865	*William Booth founds the Salvation Army.*
1870	*Foster's Education Act puts elementary education within the reach of all British children.*
1871	*Trade unions legalised in Britain.*
1884	*Greenwich meridian internationally recognised as prime meridian.*

Florence Nightingale

£5 note of 1857, produced by the techniques introduced in 1855

The Britannia of the 1857 note

On the 1855 note as well, the Chief Cashier's name was removed from the promissory clause and replaced by the words "the Bearer". The signature on the note remained that of one of the cashiers; the signature of the Chief Cashier did not replace this until 1870.

There was some criticism of the new note from the printing community. Some thought that the Bank should be employing complex machine engraving instead of the familiar design, while others recommended the use of colour photography to combat forgery. Neither of these ideas was adopted – there was no pressure to do so, because forgery was comparatively rare. There seemed to be nothing to be gained from costly design change; the Bank's notes were backed by gold and the familiar black-on-white design was accepted worldwide. Nothing should be allowed to alter the status quo as far as the design of the Bank's notes and confidence in them were concerned. Indeed, it was not until 1928 that the Bank used colour and machine engraving.

THE BANK-NOTE PRINTING-ROOM, AT THE BANK OF ENGLAND.

The Bank Note Printing Room at the Bank of England, 1854

187

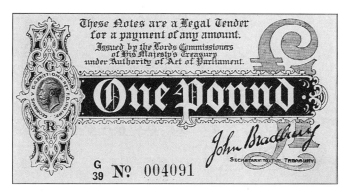

£1 and ten-shilling "Bradburys" of 1914

"Bradburys"

When World War I broke out in 1914 the situation, as far as Bank notes and gold coin in circulation was concerned, bore an eerie resemblance to the Restriction Period more than a century before: gold coins, in the form of the £1 gold sovereign and half sovereign, circulated freely (in 1797, of course, it had been the guinea and half guinea) whilst the lowest denomination Bank of England note was the familiar "white fiver". The Government was, not unreasonably, determined to ensure that the gold held by the public should be made available for the war effort, and it therefore issued notes for £1 and ten shillings to replace, the gold coins. The new lower denomination notes were a governmental rather than a Bank issue, however; they bore the facsimile signature of the Permanent Secretary to the Treasury, Sir John Bradbury, in place of that of a Bank official, and gave no hint that they were convertible into gold. Meanwhile, the Bank proffered a proof of a new £1 note based on traditional lines. It confidently promised to pay ". . . on Demand the Sum of One Pound in Standard Gold Coin . . .", but it was not accepted for two reasons: Portals, the Bank's security paper makers could not have supplied handmade paper in the quantities required, and the Scottish bankers objected to a Bank of England low denomination issue in Scotland, although they found a governmental issue acceptable. Its bold proclamation of convertibility also undoubtedly helped to seal its fate.

The new Treasury notes were a poor piece of work by a firm (Waterlow Brothers and Layton) who had never printed anything in the nature of banknotes before: the £1 notes were surface printed in black on one side only on

1893	*Thomas Hardy's* Tess of the D'Urbervilles *is published.*
1897	*Queen Victoria's Diamond Jubilee celebrations.*
1898	*Boer War begins, 10 October.*
1906	*First Labour Members of Parliament elected in Britain.*
1909	*Old age pensions introduced.*
1910	*Labour Exchanges established.*
	Death of Florence Nightingale.
1911	*National Insurance introduced.*
	British Members of Parliament are paid for the first time.
1912	*The* Titanic *disaster.*
	Death of Captain Scott and four companions while returning from the South Pole.
1914	*Britain declares war on Germany, 4 August.*
	Issue of currency notes to safeguard England's gold reserves.

£1 note of 1917

Enlarged detail

paper originally intended for postage stamps, but the new series did incorporate a portrait, albeit in profile, of the monarch, King George V – the first time this key security factor was used. The ten-shilling note was of the same format and quality, but the printing was in red and production was assisted by Thomas De La Rue & Company.

The first series was hurriedly replaced by a second that was much more akin to Bank notes, but the Bank's proprietorial instincts were aroused when it saw that the paper for the new notes carried a waved line watermark. The issue also contained a further vignette depicting St George and the Dragon.

A more sophisticated third series of Treasury notes, designed by Bertram Mackennal, came out in 1917. These notes represented a great step towards the first officially printed pictorial note in England. The £1 note bore three dominant features: St George slaying the Dragon (a design based on one that had first been introduced with the sovereign in 1817), a remodelled portrait of King George V and, on the back, as if to emphasise the identity of the issuing body, the Houses of Parliament. The ten-shilling note was similar except that a standing helmeted Britannia replaced St George.

With the war long past, the Government announced in 1925 that the export of gold would no longer be blocked, but this was only a partial return to a gold standard as there was to be no gold circulation. Under the Gold Standard Act of that year the Bank was no longer obliged to pay its notes, and the Treasury notes, in gold but was bound to sell gold per ounce in the form of 400-ounce bars to anyone who demanded it. It was hoped that this would allow gold reserves to rise to a level where a return to a full gold standard would be possible. This rise never came and the Gold Standard (Amendment) Act 1931 suspended the requirement to sell bar gold. Britain had abandoned the gold standard for ever.

Detail (the Houses of Parliament) from the back of the note

189

Colour comes to English notes

Of course, the day had to come when the country's central bank should assume responsibility for the lower denomination notes and so, in November 1928, new £1 and ten-shilling notes (Series A) were released by the Bank. They were the first coloured Bank of England notes, with intricate machine-engraved patterns overlying background tinting; they used the same Britannia as the higher denominations. The 1914 idea of a miniature version of the higher denominations was dropped in favour of designs that seemed to have evolved naturally from the currency notes they replaced: the contrast with the traditional white series could hardly have been greater.

These designs marked a dramatic change in the Bank's attitude towards its notes, opening the way for the later growth and development of the pictorial elements. The designs on the fronts of the new notes were very much alike, a denomination guilloche on the right and the 1855 Britannia on the left, separated by the promissory clause. The paper was slightly thicker than for the currency notes, a waved-line watermark was used round the edges and a helmeted Britannia, looking to the right, was centrally placed in a "window" watermark. Very significantly, the notes were undated, as they still are today.

The Threadneedle Street frontage of the Bank of England (detail from the reverse of the Series A £1 note)

1919	*League of Nations founded.*
	Einstein's theory of relativity confirmed experimentally during solar eclipse.
	First direct flight across the Atlantic by Alcock and Brown.
1920	*Degrees first open to women at Oxford University.*
1921	*Fox, Fowler and Company, the last provincial bank to issue banknotes, loses its right of issue.*
1924	*First Labour Government.*
1926	*General Strike.*
1928	*Equal Franchise Act passed, granting votes to women of age 21 and over.*
	Colour first introduced into Bank of England notes (Series A).
1931	*Final abandonment of the gold standard; Bank of England notes no longer exchangeable for gold.*

Ten-shilling Series A note,
designed by W. M. Keesey

£1 Series A note,
designed by W. M. Keesey

The £100 note of 1938

The backs of both notes were decorated with a swirling pattern of acanthus leaves, and that of the £1 note also showed the Bank's Threadneedle Street frontage. The predominant colours chosen for the new denominations – green for the £1 and red for the ten-shilling notes – set the pattern for subsequent issues. These notes continued to be issued alongside the familiar white series – the highest denomination was £1,000 – until 1940 when, for security reasons, the colour of the £1 note was changed to blue and that of the ten-shilling note to mauve. At the same time metallic thread, the invention of a Bank employee, was introduced into the paper as an additional anti-forgery device. Nevertheless counterfeiting became a serious problem during World War II, especially as a large-scale forgery operation was being carried out in Germany, and in 1943 the Bank was obliged to stop issuing notes of £10 and upwards.

At last colour printing was coming into its own, primarily because of the better protection it provided against forgery; in 1957 the first coloured £5 note (Series B) replaced the familiar "white fiver", direct descendant of the Bank's first notes of 250 years before. The predominant colour – blue – has been used for this denomination ever since. The new note was the work of an astonishingly gifted designer, Stephen Gooden, and served as a bridge between the design of the pre-war low denomination notes and the fully pictorial issues of today.

Detail drawings by Stephen Gooden for the Series B £1 (left) and £5 notes

It featured St George and the Dragon and a strikingly attractive helmeted Britannia on the front, and a lion with a double-warded key on the back. The key represented the Bank's traditional dual responsibility to protect and secure the nation's treasure and, when necessary, to release it, whilst the lion symbolising strength, is, by custom, the guardian of the treasure houses. A Britannia "window" watermark was also incorporated into this note and the waved line watermark again appeared round the edge. Sadly, Gooden died in September 1955, never having seen his design printed or issued; his superb design for £1 and ten-shilling denominations, though superb, were never used.

Planning then began for a complete new series (Series C). It was introduced in 1960 with the issue of a new green £1 note followed the year after by a reddish-brown ten-shilling note that was unmistakably the work of the same designer, Stephen Gooden's succesor Robert Austin. In order to help the visually handicapped, the dominations in the new series increased in size as they did in value. The new series broke with tradition in several ways: the portrait of the monarch appeared for the first time on a Bank of England note, a new Britannia replaced the Maclise design which had been used continuously since 1855, and the waved-line watermark was dropped in favour of a continuous patterned one. These new designs were necessary so that new printing techniques could be brought in: the pre-war £1 and ten-shilling notes could not be printed by the new reel-fed methods, since it was not feasible to align the print with the watermark in web-printed notes. A small quantity of £1 notes, which are now highly sought after by collectors, carried an inconspicuous letter "R" standing for "research machine". An unofficial feature was Austin's letter "A" worked into the Queen's portrait on the £1 note; it was spotted and deleted before the ten-shilling denomination was issued.

1933	*World Economic Conference in London.*
1939	*World War II begins; conscription introduced.*
1940	*"Battle of Britain"; City of London severely damaged by bombing.*
1941	*Military service age raised to 51; women's service became compulsory.*
1944	*6 June: "D-Day".*
1945	*End of World War II.*
	United Nations Organisation founded.
1947	*British coal industry nationalised.*
	Marriage of Princess Elizabeth and Prince Philip.
	School leaving age raised to 15.
1948	*Nationalisation of British railways and British electricity industry.*

Enlarged detail from the Series B £5 note (back)

The helmeted Britannia

The Series B £5 note

The Series C £1 note

Detail from the ten-shilling Series C note (back)

The £5 and the new £10 denominations appeared in 1964, and both were designed by Reynolds Stone, an expert letterer. His new portrait of the Queen appeared on both notes which, like the others in the series, were decorated with machine-engraving. The back of the blue £5 note featured yet another Britannia, this time modelled by the designer's daughter. The £10 note was brown and echoed Gooden's theme of a lion and key. The watermark of the highest denomination, of the series, the £10 note, consisted of a portrait of the Queen, a practice also followed in the subsequent series. This was possible because the £10 denomination was plate-printed in sheets in the traditional manner and not produced on the relatively new reel-fed machinery.

1949	Gas industry nationalised.
	North Atlantic Treaty comes into force.
1950	Death of George Bernard Shaw.
1951	Festival of Britain.
1952	Accession to the Throne of Her Majesty Queen Elizabeth II.
1953	Hillary and Tensing climb Mount Everest in an expedition led by Colonel John Hunt.
1954	London gold market reopens after 22 years.
	Roger Bannister is the first man to run a mile in under four minutes.
1956	First nuclear power station starts working in Britain.
1957	Largest radio telescope comes into operation at Jodrell Bank.
	Series B Bank notes introduced.
1958	Prince Charles becomes Prince of Wales.
1960	Series C Bank notes introduced.
1961	The New English Bible (New Testament) is published.

The New English Bible

The Britannia for the Series C £5 note (back)

The Series C £5 note (front)

Artwork for the back of the Series C £10 note

The Series C £10 note (front)

A further series of Bank of England notes was announced in March 1968. This gave the opportunity to alter the denominations, to reduce the note sizes (to economise on paper), and to introduce improved protection against forgery by means of the latest design and printing technology.

The Series D designs, issued between 1970 and 1981, were designed by Harry Eccleston, O.B.E. Eccleston, who had joined the Bank of England Printing Works in 1958, was the first full-time Artist Designer employed by the Bank; he describes his career and his approach to his work in Chapter 2. His artistic abilities and training covered a wide spectrum of disciplines including painting, portraiture, engraving, typography, illustration and graphic design – what he himself describes as "an incredible convergence of interests".

Harry Eccleston is a graduate of Birmingham College of Art and later of the Royal College of Art's Engraving School, where he trained under Robert Austin; assisted by the artists, engravers, scientists and other skilled craftsmen who make up the design team, he has raised English banknotes to previously unattained levels of design, craftsmanship, aesthetics and, above all, security. His greatest influence on the Series D notes, and the aspect of their design which sets them apart from all previous English notes, has been in the field of portraiture. Two royal portraits were produced for the series, as well as a new design for Britannia, and the reverse of each denomination carries a portrait of a distinguished historical figure. All the portraits were engraved by Alan Dow of Bradbury Wilkinson, except for that on the £1 note which was engraved by David Wicks (an employee of the Bank of England Printing Works).

The first of the new series to be issued was the £20 note, in July 1970. The portrait of the Queen in state robes is not enclosed in a frame but blends into the background with no clear boundaries. The front carries a vignette of St George and the Dragon and the back shows William Shakespeare, drawn from the memorial statue in Westminster Abbey, with the balcony scene from "*Romeo and Juliet*" shown in the background. The note is predominantly purple, with gold, blue and green tints. In 1984, two significant alterations were made to this note: the security thread was to appear at intervals on the surface, through a process known as "windowing", and the original watermark of the Queen's portrait was changed to one portraying Shakespeare – the watermark of the Queen is only used for the highest-denomination note in this series and the £50 note was by then well established.

November 1971 saw the issue of the £5 note; again its predominant colour was blue. A portrait of the Duke of Wellington appears on the back of this note, taken from a painting in Apsley House, his London home, together with a battle scene based on the Battle of Fuentes de Onoro which was fought during the Peninsular Campaign. The central vignette on the front shows a Winged Victory, a popular symbol of military prowess at that time. The note was printed at first on a sheet-fed plate press, but since 1976 it has been web-printed. Intaglio is used on the front and offset lithography on the back, which is marked with the letter "L" to denote the change from an earlier printed intaglio back. In 1987 the original security thread was replaced by a wider one.

1963	*The Great Train Robbery – more than £2½ million is stolen from the Glasgow to London Mail Train.*
1965	*Death of Sir Winston Churchill.*
1968	*First- and second-class (two tier) postal system introduced.*
1969	*Abolition of the death penalty.*
1970	*Series D Bank notes introduced.*
1971	*Decimal currency introduced.*
1973	*Britain joins European Economic Community.*
	Value Added Tax introduced in Britain.

Series D £20 note (front)

Series D £5 note (front)

Artwork for the Wellington portrait (Series D £5 note)

Artwork for the "Winged Victory" vignette
(Series D £5 note)

The £10 note, issued in February 1975 and predominantly brown in colour, uses the same portrait of the Queen as does the £20 note. A portrait of Florence Nightingale, a blend of images from three photographs, appears on the back with a background scene showing her tending to sick soldiers in the barracks hospital at Scutari. The lily symbol on the front is one that she is said to have used. Windowed thread, similar to that in the £20 note, was introduced into the £10 note in 1987.

Artwork for the Nightingale portrait (Series D £10 note)

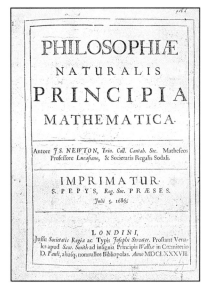

Title page of Newton's Principia, *which appears on the reverse of the Series D £1 note*

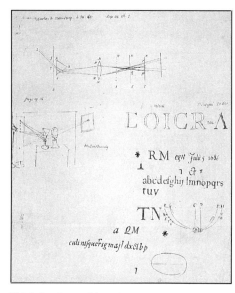

Trial sketches and lettering for the Series D £1 note

The portrait of the Queen on the green £1 note, issued in February 1978, is the same as on the £5 note. The design of the vignette on the front was taken from a token commemorating Sir Isaac Newton and includes a caduceus, a cornucopia and an olive branch. Unlike all the other notes in the series this note carried only one serial number, printed in the bottom right-hand corner. Newton's portrait on the reverse showed him seated with a copy of his book *Principia* or *Mathematical Principles of Natural Philosophy and Systems of the World* open at the page concerned with the elliptical movement of the planets, together with a machine-engraved pattern representing the solar system. This note was printed entirely by offset on a sheet-fed machine from 1978 until 1981, when it was transferred to the web process and the front printed by intaglio and the back by offset lithography. The note was replaced by a coin early in 1985, and ceased to be legal tender in 1988.

1976	*Concorde commences supersonic passenger service.*
	Worst drought in Britain for 500 years.
1979	*Margaret Thatcher, Britain's first woman Prime Minister is elected.*
1981	*First London Marathon run.*

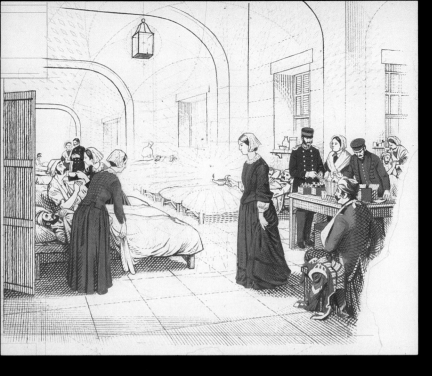

Series D £10 note (front)

Artwork for reverse of the Series D £10 note

Series D £1 note (front)

Master portrait for reverse of the Series D £1 note

Artwork for guilloche for Series D £50 note based on Grinling Gibbons' wood carvings in the South Choir Aisle of St Paul's Cathedral

The final denomination in this series appeared in March 1981. The £50 note uses the portrait of the Queen produced for the £10 and £20 denominations, and its colour is a mixture of olive green, brown and grey. The vignette next to the portrait shows "a phoenix arising from the flames" and other patterns on the front represent design features of St Paul's Cathedral. The portrait of Sir Christopher Wren on the reverse was drawn by Harry Eccleston from contemporary portraits by J. B. Clostermann and Sir Godfrey Kneller; Wren is shown against a background of a view of St. Paul's from the River Thames based on a 1749 engraving by S. & M. Buck. This was produced by Roger Withington, the Bank's current Artist Designer. The edge of the security thread in the £50 note was originally contoured in a regular pattern which could face to either side, produced on microprocessor-controlled laser slitting equipment made by the U.K. Atomic Energy Authority. In 1988, the colours of the note were altered and the contoured thread was replaced by windowed thread as in the £10 and £20 notes as a further defence against forgery.

Each note in the series was meticulously researched, with every aspect of the subject's life being explored for source material to illustrate Eccleston's design themes. These were a skilful amalgamation of the security aspects of intaglio and offset printing, typographic illustration and portraiture, which with the growth in the the number of notes needed for circulation must today be combined with high production speed. First class hand-drawing and engraving, reproduced by intaglio printing and enhanced by machine-engraved patterns, remain the best deterrents against forgery while modern technology provides the means for accurate and fast reproduction. The last eighty years have seen the greatest change in English banknotes since the Bank of England was founded, from documents carrying little more than essential phrases and numbers to notes that are overwhelmingly pictorial, with the minimum of wording dominated by representational artwork and abstract security printing.

The Series D Britannia

1982	*20 August: Bank of England suspends minimum lending rate.*
1983	*21 April: £1 coin introduced.*
1986	*Anglo-French agreement on Channel Tunnel rail link.*
	27 October: "Big Bang" in London: deregulation of the City's financial system.
1987	*Britain's worst storm for nearly 300 years devastates southern England.*
1988	*The Chartered Institute of Bankers' paper money collection, comprising over 30,000 items, is formally handed over to the British Museum on indefinite loan.*

£1 coin (reverse)

Master portrait for the Series D £50 note

The Series D £50 note (front)

Master drawing of the Phoenix for the Series D £50 note, based on the Caius Cibber carving on St Paul's and Wren's Phoenix for the Monument in London

Litt. D. Nō. *11164.*   10. Thlr.

Zehen Reichs Thaler

Churfürstl. Sächsl. Cassen

Werden bey denen Churfürstl. Stuben

Maasgabe des Edicts, d. d. den 6 May 1772.

Dresden, den Sechsten May, 17

Litt. D. Nō. *1116*

Schrondt Waldorf

Commissarius.

Electorate of Saxony ten-Reichsthaler Cassen-Billet of 1772

GERMANY

Following the example of the Royal Prussian Giro- und Lehnbank in Berlin six years before, the Electorate of Saxony issued its first notes in 1772; 783,750 of these Saxon Cassen-Billets were printed with a total value of 1,500,000 thaler. There were six denominations, from 1 thaler (letter A) to 100 thaler (letter F).

The designers of the notes thoroughly understood the importance of deterring counterfeiters, and used several well-tried methods: intaglio printing from engraved copper plates, watermarked paper and a variety of lettering styles, together with handwritten numbers and the personal signatures of the commissioner and the book-keeper.

MILESTONES IN GERMAN BANKNOTE PRINTING

Act of Parliament of the 11 Aug 1803 against forgery of foreign bills of exchange etc.

The Pommersche Ritterschaftliche Privat-Bank, Stettin, opened on 5 January 1825, and immediately issued its first 1 million thaler notes, which had the same value as the Prussian Treasury bills. Stone engraving was used for printing. The backs of the notes showed the town of Stettin, with a border carrying various initials and names, to make counterfeiting more difficult, and a reference to an English Act of Parliament against the forgery of foreign money – this was added as a warning to English counterfeiters, who had been making a comfortable profit out of fake Prussian bills.

One-Reichsthaler bill issued by the Pommersche Ritterschaftliche Privat-Bank, Stettin, undated (1824–25), back

Dieser von der ritterschaftlichen Privatbank in Pommern ausgefertigte Bankschein wird, zu dem obigen Betrage, in ihren Comtoirs zu jeder Zeit einem jeden Inhaber vollständig realisirt. Annehmbar auch in den Königl. Cassen in Pommern bei Entrichtung der öffentlichen Abgaben zu ⅘ des Courant-Betrages derselben, auch dabei anrechenbar auf das Tresorschein-Pflichtheil.

Pommerscher Bankschein.

The "three-dimensional" note

Jakob Degen's pioneering guilloche machine, developed in Vienna in 1810, opened the way to the elaborate equipment of today; subsequent technical advances make it possible for engravers to produce realistic *bas-relief* effects. The five-gulden note illustrated was printed by the Frankfurt firm of Carl Naumann, whose designer revelled in the new style and covered the whole of the reverse with relief engraving, of which the large numeral, with its confident flourish, is especially successful.

Duchy of Nassau five-gulden note of 1847, back

Printing on both sides

The Frankfurter Bank's 35-gulden bank bill dated 1 January 1855, produced by Carl Naumann, represented the state-of-the-art technology of the day; the two intaglio-printed profiles of Francofordia were taken from a three-dimensional original. The girl's head forming the central portrait motif on the front of the note is also printed on the reverse on a guilloched background, in exact register with the front. The denomination of 35 gulden was chosen because it corresponded to 20 thaler.

The prison wall

The arrangement of motifs on the Gera Bank's ten-thaler banknote dated 15 January 1856 is characteristic of notes produced by the Leipzig firm of Giesecke & Devrient. The face was printed by the letterpress process, and the allegorical group on the reverse was intaglio-printed.

The bottom margin on the front shows an inscription on a wall linking the two towers of a prison. Two lines of text, headed "Penalty order", are shown twice – once right way up, and then upside-down.

The order reads "Whosoever alters or forges the notes of the bank, or knowingly utters forged notes or aids in their utterance, will be liable to the penalty provided by law."

Ten-thaler banknote issued by the Gera Bank in 1856:
(right) back, and
(below) detail from front

206

Die Frankfurter Bank

bezahlt gegen diesen Bankschein

35 GULDEN

IN BAAREM GELDE.

Frankfurt M.   1 Januar 1855.

Der Director   *Der Subdirector*

Litera D. Serie II.   Fol. 210 N° 2998

35   **35**

FÜNF & DREISSIG   FÜNF & DREISSIG

Für die Controle:

Multicolour background printing

The Royal Prussian State Printing Works in Berlin used an interesting anti-counterfeiting device on the front of its one-thaler Kassen-Anweisung of 1856. The background consists of 53 lines of text, in which the penalty order against forging is repeated over and over again. The groups of letters are printed in five different colours, giving a honeycomb effect. This made the note almost impossible to counterfeit, but so many notes were spoilt during printing because of the complexity of the printing technique that the design was abandoned. Many years passed before German printers learnt how to print multicoloured backgrounds on both sides of a note with perfect registration, using a process that combined a range of steps into a single pass.

One-thaler Kassen-Anweisung of the Kingdom of Prussia, dated 15 December 1856, front

A portrait watermark in a broad margin

The Reich Printing Works in Berlin, the successor to the Royal Prussian State Printing Works, was established in 1879, and the 100-mark Reichsbank banknote illustrated is characteristic of its output. The lettering on the front of the note appears against the imperial insignia, with the Habsburg eagles and the heads of Mercury and Ceres on either side; on the back a crowned and armed Germania guards the German coast, with symbols of trade, industry and agriculture at her feet and a distant view of a fleet of warships beyond.

   The note was designed by Friedrich Wanderer, and engraved by Carl Strassgürtl. The motifs were intaglio-printed on handmade banknote paper; the broad margin was left unprinted, but is watermarked with a portrait of Kaiser William I.

100-mark Reichsbank banknote issued in 1908, front and back

Mirror-image portraits

The 100-mark Reichsbank banknote was designed by Professor Oskar Hermann Werner Hadank and produced by multicolour letterpress printing. For security reasons Hadank introduced a pair of mirror-image portraits of the Bamberg Horseman, but critics of the time regarded the inversion of the portrait as artistically indefensible, and Hadank's idea was abandoned. Later notes used portrait heads from the paintings of Dürer, Holbein and others.

100-mark Reichsbank banknote issued in 1920, front

A special type of banknote paper

Even during the chaos that followed World War I, no-one wanted to do away with security features in banknotes. The designers of the 100-trillion-mark Reichsbank banknote – the highest denomination ever issued by the Reichsbank – included an elaborate running watermark on the right of the paper, representing stylised thistle leaves, and heightened its effect with a brown stripe running through the paper and with embedded purple and green threads in the wine-red part of the design. The production of the note required the co-operation of the Reich Printing Works with no fewer than six other printers.

100 trillion-mark Reichsbank banknote issued in 1923

Watermark

210

Five-Deutsche mark banknote issued by the Bank deutscher Länder in 1948 (second issue), front

The first security thread

In 1948 the Bank deutscher Länder faced something of an emergency. Faked five-Deutsche mark banknotes were being produced in large numbers, and a new note had become an urgent necessity. At the time, however, no banknote paper could be produced in the Federal Republic of Germany, no banknotes could be printed and there was no possibility of minting a replacement coin, and the Bank commissioned Thomas De La Rue & Co. Ltd of London to print the new notes.

The banknote was designed by the graphic artist Max Bittrof, who took as his theme the Greek myth of Europa and the bull. The front of the banknote, which was intaglio-printed, illustrates the abduction of an apparently compliant Europa by Zeus in his bull persona, and Bittrof also used Europa's head as the watermark. After the Bank's experience with the earlier note the need for enhanced security was all too evident, and the Europa note was the first German banknote to carry a security thread.

In 1955, the Federal Printing Works took over production of the banknotes.

Grand Duchy of Baden

The notes of the Baden Government's first issue of paper money are among the most handsome of the time. The two-gulden note dated 1 July 1849 was designed by Ludwig Kachel (1791–1878), the plates were made by Carl Naumann and the paper was watermarked with plant designs. "Blind" (embossed) stamps were used as a protection against forgery; as a further protection, the back of the note is an exact mirror image of the front, printed with perfect registration.

The Act of 30 April 1874 allowed all Government notes in gulden and thaler to be converted into Reichskassenscheine (cash bills) valued in the mark.

"Blind" stamp

| 1848 | Communist Manifesto by Karl Marx and Friedrich Engels. March Revolution in Germany. Thirty-nine members of the "German Confederation" begin to issue paper money. |
| 1852 | Foundation of the Giesecke & Devrient Typographic Institute in Leipzig. |

March revolution

Serie G. 1.

№ 717,841.

Zwei Gulden

Großherzoglich Badiſches Papier-Geld, welches bei allen Zahlungen an Badiſche
Staats-Caſſen im vollen Nennwerthe, gleich dem im Landes-Münzfuße geprägten
groben Silbergelde, angenommen und von der Einlöſungs-Caſſe in Carlsruhe auf
Sicht gegen grobe Silber-Münzen ausgewechſelt wird.

Nach dem Geſetz vom 3. März 1849.

Carlsruhe, den 1. Juli 1849.
Großh. Badiſche
General-Staats-Caſſe:

№ 717,841.

Serie G. 1.

Zwei Gulden

Großherzoglich Badiſches Papier-Geld, welches bei allen Zahlungen an Badiſche
Staats-Caſſen im vollen Nennwerthe, gleich dem im Landes-Münzfuße geprägten
groben Silbergelde, angenommen und von der Einlöſungs-Caſſe in Carlsruhe auf
Sicht gegen grobe Silber-Münzen ausgewechſelt wird.

Nach dem Geſetz vom 3. März 1849.

Carlsruhe, den 1. Juli 1849.
Großh. Badiſche
General-Staats-Caſſe:

Danziger Privat-Actien-Bank, Danzig

The ten-thaler banknote dated 1 July 1857 was printed on watermarked paper and the denominations on the face were in German, English and French. Danzig (now Gdansk), once the capital of West Prussia, stands at the mouth of the River Weichsel on the Baltic, and the reverse of the note carries an intaglio-printed allegorical motif celebrating the city's position and power. A river nymph links hands with a mermaid under the protection of a crowned sea-goddess; Mercury, ready to fly at her bidding, his winged staff and the anchor symbolise trade and shipping. This banknote is one of many produced by Giesecke & Devrient.

In 1892, the Danziger Privat-Actien-Bank waived its right of issue.

Details with the denominations in English and French

1857   *Death of the poet Joseph von Eichendorff.*
1862   *Otto von Bismarck becomes Ministerpräsident of Prussia and Foreign Minister.*

10 DIX ÉCUS

10 TEN THALERS

Die
Danziger Privat-Actien-Bank
zahlt

ZEHN THALER

dem Inhaber dieser Note.

Danzig, den 1. Juli 1857.

Der Verwaltungsrath:

Der vollziehende Director:

Nach § 17 des Statuts löst die Bank diese Note bei Präsentation in klingend Courant ein; nach § 20 kann ein Aufruf zur Einlösung oder zum Umtausch erfolgen.

Wer die Noten verfälscht oder nachmacht, oder nachgemachte ode. verfälschte Noten wissentlich verbreitet oder verbreiten hilft, wird nach den Landesgesetzen bestraft.

Lit. A.

No. 10601.

DANZIGER PRIVAT-ACTIEN-BANK

LEIPZIG, GIESECKE & DEVRIENT, TYP. INST.

Issue of the Royal Bavarian
Staats-Schuldentilgungs-Commission

The 50-gulden bill was issued because of the state's need for money after the Austro-Bavarian war against Prussia in 1866, and later to finance the 1870 Franco–Prussian war.

The Bavarian coat of arms on the front of the note is flanked to the left and right by medallions showing the Muses of music and painting, architecture and sculpture. The head of the symbolic figure of Bavaria is shown twice, facing right and left, and between the two are the facsimile signatures of the Deputy Speaker of the Board, Sutner, and the Land Diet Commissioners, Dr von Bayer and Graf von Hegnenberg Dux. The reverse of the note shows a bust of Bavaria, accompanied by allegorical figures representing the Danube, Isar, Rhine and Main rivers.

1864	War of Prussia and Austria against Denmark for dominance of Schleswig-Holstein.
1866	War of Prussia against Austria (and the German Confederation).
	Austria is defeated; the German Confederation comes to an end.
1870	The Franco-Prussian War begins.

Allegorical figures: music and painting, architecture and sculpture

The first Reichsbank issue

The foundation of the Reich was quickly followed by the introduction of a new currency unit, the mark: three marks were equivalent to one thaler, and twelve marks to seven gulden.

The Banking Act of 14 March 1875 authorised the Reichsbank to issue banknotes denominated 100, 200, 500, 1,000 and multiples of 1,000 marks, but the 200- and 500-mark banknotes were never issued. The 100-mark banknote carried the facsimile signatures of the first President of the Reichsbank, von Dechend (previously President of the Preussische Bank), and the other members of the Board: Boese, von Rotth, Gallenkamp, Herrmann, Koch and von Koenen. These notes remained in circulation until 5 June 1925.

The old Reichsbank building in Berlin

1871	*After the end of the War, the German states join to make up the German Reich. The King of Prussia is proclaimed Kaiser William I in Versailles.*
1876	*Inauguration of the Reichsbank in Berlin.*

100-mark Reichsbank banknote issued in 1876, front

Detail from the back

The Reichsschuldenverwaltung issue

Detail "Naked Little Boy"

After the Deutsche Reich was founded, the Act of 30 April 1874 allowed for an amount of Reichskassenscheine to be issued in the mark and circulated in the Federal States of the Reich in numbers based on their respective populations; they were to replace the gulden and thaler notes in circulation at that time. At first it was planned to put 120 million marks worth into circulation, but the final figure was higher. Reichskassenscheine were not legal tender and only public cash offices were required to accept them at their nominal value.

The 20-mark bill was printed on special paper, called "Willcox paper" after its American inventor, and given statutory protection. It was made by working coloured threads into the pulp during the papermaking process, and was watermarked with the figure "20".

Tenders were invited for the design of the note, and the selection was subject to the Kaiser's personal approval; even royal favour, however, failed to prevent some people being shocked by the nudity of the curly-headed little boys on the front. The notes were withdrawn at the end of 1910.

1881	"League of the Three Emperors" between the German Reich, Austria-Hungary and Russia.
1882	Robert Koch discovers the tuberculosis bacillus.
1884	Ottmar Mergenthaler invents the linotype machine.
1888	"Year of the Three Emperors": death of Kaiser William I, 99-day reign of Kaiser Frederick III, accession of Kaiser William II. Heinrich Hertz discovers the waves named after him, the basis of modern radio technology.
1893	Rudolf Diesel develops the engine named after him.
1898	Construction of the Braun tube by Karl Ferdinand Braun – the basis of today's television tube.

REICHS KASSEN SCHEIN

Gesetz vom 30. April 1874

Zwanzig Mark.

Berlin den 10. Januar 1882.

Reichsschuldenverwaltung.

Wer Reichskassenscheine nachmacht oder verfälscht, oder nachgemachte oder verfälschte
Reichskassenscheine wissentlich in Verkehr bringt, wird nach §§ 146 bis 149 des Strafs-
gesetzbuchs vom 15. Mai 1871 bestraft.

D·Nr 481872

20

The five-mark Reichskassenschein used paper with the watermark "5" and was designed by Alexander Zick (1845–1907). The front shows Germania with a little boy and symbols of shipping, mechanical engineering, trade and agriculture, while on the reverse a winged dragon, breathing fire, protects a hoard of treasure. Issued in April 1906, the note was in circulation until 5 June 1925.

Reichsbank issues

The Act of 20 February 1906 authorised the Reichsbank to "print and issue 20- and 50-mark banknotes". The 1920 banknote was designed by Professor Arthur Kampf and used paper with the watermark "50". The front carries an eye-catching portrait of a radiant young girl, her head wreathed with roses and her arms loaded with fruit; on the reverse, a farmworker and an artisan symbolise agriculture and industry. The note was circulated until 5 June 1925.

1900	The civil code (Bürgerliches Gesetzbuch, BGB) and the commercial code (Handelsgesetzbuch, HGB) come into force.
1902	Inauguration of the Berlin underground railway.
1910	All Reichsbank banknotes are declared legal tender.
	The total population of the German Reich reaches 64.9 million.
1914	Outbreak of World War I; the Reichsbank suspends the exchange of Reichsbank banknotes for gold.
1915	Food ration cards are introduced; nearly all foodstuffs are rationed.
1916	The Reich Printing Office gives private printers a share in banknote manufacturing.
1917	Famine in Germany following the "Turnip Winter" of 1916–17.
1919	Signing of the Treaty of Versailles.

Five-mark Reichskassenschein: detail from the back

*Detail from the front of
50-mark Reichsbank banknote*

The 50-trillion-mark Reichsbank banknote was issued in March 1924, as uncontrolled inflation swung into a dizzy spiral; following the Banking Act of 30 August 1924 the Reichsbank called in all banknotes valued in marks, and from 5 March 1925 onwards exchanged them at a rate of one trillion (1 million million) marks to one Reichsmark. The banknote, which carried a portrait of the Nuremberg councillor Jakob Muffel, was ephemeral: from 6 July 1925 all Reichsbank banknotes valued in marks were worthless.

The portrait of Jakob Muffel was used again on the front of the 100-Deutsche mark banknote of the Bank deutscher Länder almost 25 years later. On the reverse of the note is a view of part of the old town of Nuremberg.

In official circulation until 31 July 1965, the banknote may still be exchanged at the Deutsche Bundesbank.

1921	*Nobel prize for physics awarded to Albert Einstein.*
1922	*Banknotes are printed on rotary presses from reels of paper.*
1923	*Runaway inflation in Germany: at times, more than 7,500 people are employed in money operations at the Reich Printing Office; 84 printers are involved directly and another 60 printers indirectly in banknote printing.*
	Introduction of the Rentenmark: 1 trillion (1,000,000,000,000) marks = 1 Rentenmark.
1926	*Germany becomes a member of the League of Nations.*
1927	*Compulsory unemployment insurance introduced in Germany.*
1929	*The airship* Graf Zeppelin *flies around the world.*
	First television broadcast in Berlin.
1931	*Bank crash: a run on the counters results in the insolvency of the Danat-Bank (Darmstadt and National Bank).*
1932	*More than 6 million people are unemployed in Germany.*
1933	*Paul von Hindenburg appoints Adolf Hitler Chancellor. Hjalmar Schacht becomes President of the Reichsbank. Schacht finances job creation measures and rearmament.*
1934	*Adolf Hitler becomes head of state as Führer and Chancellor.*
1935	*Introduction of universal conscription and compulsory labour service.*
	The four remaining private note-issuing banks lose their issuing privilege.
1936	*IVth Winter Olympic Games held in Garmisch-Partenkirchen; XIth Summer Olympic Games held in Berlin.*

Albert Einstein

100-Deutsche mark banknote, Bank deutscher Länder issue, front

Back

Deutsche Rentenbank bills

The regulations for the establishment of the Deutsche Rentenbank of 15 October 1923 provided for the issue of Rentenbank bills, so that two kinds of paper money were circulating in Germany: Reichsbank banknotes and Rentenbank bills. Only the Reichsbank banknotes were legal tender and had by law to be accepted in payment of a debt. Rentenbank bills, on the other hand, were merely legally permitted means of payment.

The 50-Rentenmark Rentenbank bill honoured the Prussian statesman Baron vom Stein (1757–1831), who was a leading opponent of Napoleon. The front carried a head-and-shoulders portrait of vom Stein, and his portrait also appears in the watermark.

The Reichsbank wartime issue

The five-Reichsmark Reichsbank banknote of August 1942 carried a broad unprinted margin watermarked with the number "5". The young man's head on the front is the work of Professor Josef Seger. The reverse was designed by W. Riemer and shows Braunschweig Cathedral with the nearby Lion Monument, flanked by a peasant woman and a workman symbolising agriculture and manual trades. The banknote was withdrawn on 20 June 1948.

1938	Austria incorporated into the German Reich.
	Munich Settlement between Germany, Great Britain, Italy and France.
1939	Soviet–German non-aggression pact.
	Outbreak of World War II.
1943	Turning point of World War II after Stalingrad.
1944	20 July: German officers attempt to murder Hitler, but the plot fails.
1945	End of World War II, Potsdam Conference: Germany is divided into zones of occupation.
	Rotary press used to produce 1,200,000 copies per hour of an eight-page newspaper.
1946	Nuremberg trials of war criminals.
	First Volkswagen Beetle produced.
1948	Foundation of the Bank deutscher Länder (BdL) as the central note-issuing authority.
	Currency reform in the western zones of Germany and in West Berlin: 10 RM = 1 DM.

Volkswagen

Detail from the back

Allegory of agriculture

Allegory of manual trades

The currency reform of 1948

20-Deutsche mark banknote issued by the Bank deutscher Länder, 1948 series, detail from front

The German currency was reformed yet again in 1948; from 21 June the new currency unit was the Deutsche mark, which was divided into 100 pfennigs. The new series of banknotes was produced by the American Bank Note Company, New York, and the notes were intaglio-printed on unwatermarked paper . The front of the ten-Deutsche mark banknote shows an allegorical group symbolising manual trades; symbols of industry, agriculture and science are carried by the 20-, 50- and 100-Deutsche mark banknotes.

At the same time, other currency reform banknotes were produced by the Bureau of Engraving and Printing in Washington, which were marked "1948 series" except the 20- and 50-Deutsche mark banknotes. The denominations were one-half, one, two, five, 20 and 50 Deutsche marks and all of them were produced using only offset printing; they were thus relatively easy to forge.

None of the currency reform banknotes carries the name of an issuing authority.

West Berlin was not included in the West German currency area and the notes issued in West Berlin were provided with an additional round B-stamp or B-perforation; a few banknotes carried both.

1949	The Basic Law for the Federal Republic of Germany is proclaimed.
1950	Germany joins the Council of Europe.
1951	Peace prize of the German book trade awarded to Albert Schweitzer.
1952	The Federal Republic of Germany joins the International Monetary Fund and the World Bank.
1953	17 June workers' uprising in East Berlin and in the German Democratic Republic.
1955	The Federal Republic of Germany joins NATO.
1957	Saarland becomes the tenth Land of the Federal Republic of Germany.
	The Deutsche Bundesbank Act comes into force.

100-Deutsche mark banknote: detail from front

Deutsche Bundesbank Issue

Portrait of Sebastian Münster
by Christoph Amberger
(about 1500—62)

The 100-Deutsche mark Bundesbank banknote with portrait watermark, dated 2 January 1960, went into circulation for the first time on 26 February 1962, bearing the facsimile signatures of the Governor and the Deputy Governor of the Deutsche Bundesbank (who at that time were Karl Blessing and Dr Troeger, respectively). There have since been issues in 1970 (signed by Karl Klasen and Otmar Emminger), 1977 (signed by Emminger and Pöhl) and 1980 (signed by Pöhl and Professor Schlesinger). The portrait is taken from a painting by Christoph Amberger of the cosmographer Sebastian Münster; the back of the banknote is dominated by the spread eagle.

The 100-Deutsche mark Bundesbank banknote was one of a series with seven denominations, designed by the graphic artist Hermann Eidenbenz, produced by Giesecke & Devrient.

1958	*Convertibility of the Deutsche mark.*
	The EEC and Euratom Treaties come into force.
1961	*The Berlin Wall built between East and West Berlin.*

Design by Hermann Eidenbenz

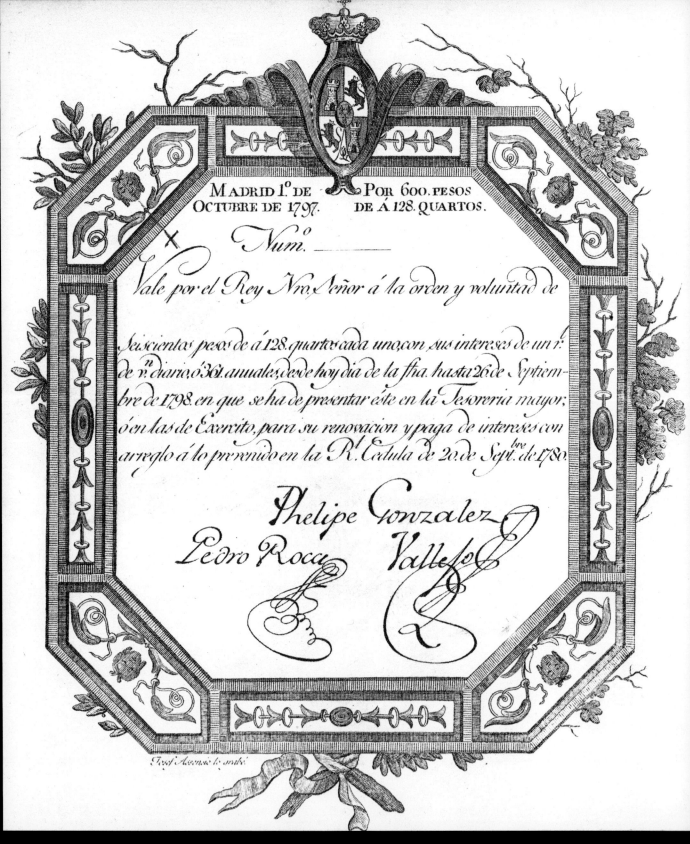

MADRID 1º DE OCTUBRE DE 1797. POR 600. PESOS DE Á 128. QUARTOS.

Numº ————

Vale por el Rey Nro. Señor á la orden y voluntad de

Seiscientos pesos de á 128. quartos cada uno, con sus intereses de un rl de vn diario, ó 36 l. anuales, desde hoy dia de la ffa. hasta 26 de Septiembre de 1798. en que se ha de presentar éste en la Tesoreria mayor; ó en las de Exercito, para su renovacion y paga de intereses con arreglo á lo prevenido en la Rl. Cedula de 20. de Sepbre. de 1780.

Phelipe Gonzalez
Pedro Roca   Vallejo

Josef Asensio lo grabó

600-peso banknote of 1797

SPAIN

LIBRO
PRIMERO
De Acuerdos reservados de
las Juntas particulares de
la Dirección del Banco Nacional de SAN CARLOS,
creado por S.M. el Rey nuestro Señor DON CARLOS
TERCERO en Real Ce-
dula de 2 de Junio de
el Año 1782.

MILESTONES IN
SPANISH BANKNOTE PRINTING

Early Spanish banknotes

The royal notes issued in 1780 by the Banco de San Carlos (1782–1829) were Spain's first official paper money, but the first banknotes, known as *cédulas*, were not circulated until 1783. The *cédulas* were technically very simple: they were printed only on the front, in single colour intaglio on a screw press, with a different colour and a different border for each denomination. The number was handwritten on the top left-hand corner, and the watermark in the paper combined figures and letters. As an additional safeguard, each banknote was individually signed and initialled by the General Cashier, the General Accountant and the Director. These *cédulas* were printed in the Intaglio Section of the Royal Printing Works, which specialised in high-value documents. The first issue is dated 1 March 1783; the note illustrated is a reprint made fifteen years later.

The notes issued in 1835 by the Banco Español de San Fernando, which succeeded the Banco de San Carlos, were technically similar to those of 1783 and 1798. Their borders were more elaborate, however, and included

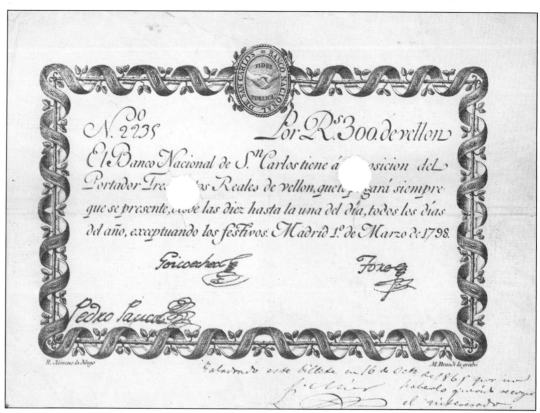

Banknote for 300 reales de vellon, issued in 1798 by the Banco de San Carlos

234

the warning "death penalty to forgers", while the raggedly cut left-hand edge afforded a check on authenticity. The issues of the 1840s also had intricate borders and handwritten signatures and initials with, as an additional security feature, "blind" stamps at the four corners.

The Banco de Isabel II was created by a royal decree of 25 January 1844 but, because the Banco de San Fernando retained the privilege of issuing banknotes, the new bank's paper money had to be called by the old name of *cédulas*. For the first time on Spanish banknotes, a portrait head – the Queen's – appeared in the watermark. A few security features from earlier issues (handwritten signatures, initials and numbers, and "blind" stamps) were retained but the notes were printed only by lithography, except for the innovation of some engraving on the reverse. The same design was used for the whole series, but with a different colour for each denomination.

After the Banco de Isabel II merged with the Banco de San Fernando in 1847, a new issue was produced in the bank's premises. The new notes were a noticeable improvement on the old, with heavier paper, much more intricate intaglio borders on the front and, for the first time, lithographic printing on the reverse. They carried three printed signatures, which were later hand-initialled by the signatories, but this practice was abandoned in later issues.

Banknote for 10,000 reales de vellon, issued in 1844 by the Banco de Isabel II

Banknote for 4,000 reales de vellon, issued in 1847 by the Banco de San Fernando, front and back

Forgery was thriving, however, and the London firm of Saunders was asked to manufacture a new series, to include banknotes of 500, 1,000, 2,000 and 4,000 reales. The front was printed in black intaglio, with the rosettes and outer border produced with a cycloid machine and acid-etched. For the first time, the number was printed in letterpress. The back was white, but the front was of a different colour for each denomination. Good-quality paper was used, and the watermark contained the name of the bank and a line drawing.

Banknote for 500 reales de vellon, issued in 1850 by the Banco de San Fernando

First issues from the Bank of Spain

The 1856 issue made by the newly created Bank of Spain was also printed by Saunders. These were the first Spanish banknotes to be printed in several colours; the value of the note was printed in letterpress in the centre of the design in a different colour for each denomination. The name of the issuing branch (Valencia in the note illustrated) and the words "El Director" were also printed in letterpress in another colour.

Banknote for 4,000 reales de vellon, issued in 1856 by the Valencia branch of the Bank of Spain

Banknote for 4,000 reales de vellon, issued in 1862

The 1862 issue, again produced by Saunders, was technically important in that it introduced some features that are still used in banknotes today. On the front, the micrometric background was printed in lithography and the border in letterpress, with high-quality engravings printed in black intaglio. The back was printed in two colour letterpress. The watermark was still very simple, however, consisting of the words "Banco de España" and the nominal value in figures and letters.

Saunders also produced the beautiful and technically advanced issue of 1 January 1866, the fronts of which were printed in both lithography and intaglio. This was the first issue launched after the Monetary Reform Act of 16 June 1864 introduced the escudo as the new unit of currency; together with the 1856 and 1862 issues, it was presented at the Paris Exhibition.

Ten-escudo note of 1866 (detail)

Since the forgery scare of 1850, all Spanish banknotes had been printed in London. There were clear drawbacks in this dependence on a foreign industry, however, and the bank decided to begin manufacturing them in Spain. By January 1868, an engraving and printing workshop was operating in the bank's premises, producing some 2,000 banknotes daily. This issue consisted of a single series of 100-escudo notes, of which 100,000 were printed. They were technically simple, being printed in lithography without any background. As in the issue of 1 May 1862, the words "Banco de España" appeared vertically in the watermark on either side of the note, with the value in words and figures in the centre.

100-escudo note of 1868 (details)

New issues were launched every year from 1868 to 1873, among which the issue of 31 December 1871 is outstanding: it marked the point at which banknotes began to resemble those of today. The three banknotes of this series bore the portrait of a distinguished person on the left and etched or machine-engraved vignettes on the lower right-hand corner. The banknotes were printed in three colour intaglio on lithographic backgrounds; the backs were left unprinted. The paper, which incorporated a worsted fibre, was watermarked across its whole surface with a motif consisting of a central circle with the head of Mercury and the value of each note (in figures) encircled by a chain.

50-escudo note of 1871

The sole bank of issue

The Bank of Spain's workshop soon became unable to meet the increasing demand from traders for banknotes, and between 1876 and 1884 both the workshop and the American Bank Note Company of New York were producing Spanish notes. But although the bank reorganised its manufacturing department and provided it with new resources, the standard of the notes it produced was not high and forgeries again became common. In addition, in the first years of this century, the bank's workshop suffered a crisis from which it never recovered.

1,000-peseta note of 1876

The 1,000-peseta note dated 12 July 1876, made by the American Note Company, was a technical achievement at the time. On the front the foreground was printed totally in black intaglio and the background in two-colour letterpress. It included both etched and hand-engraved vignettes and, for the first time on a Spanish banknote, a guilloche produced by a geometric lathe. The back was printed in single-colour letterpress. The outer border was a white line, also produced by the geometric lathe, and there was no watermark.

The intaglio-printed 1,000-peseta note dated 1 May 1895 was also notable. Among Domingo Martinez Aparisi's engravings on the front was a remarkable portrait of the Count of Cabarrus, taken from a painting by Goya. The papers contained a strip and lettering that could be seen when it was held up to the light. The watermark showed a classical head in a rosette, the amount of the banknote in figures near the bottom and vertically in the centre, and the letters B.E. (for "Banco de España").

1,000-peseta note of 1895

Bradbury Wilkinson of London were first commissioned by the Bank of Spain when a new issue was urgently needed in 1906, and remained its sole supplier until 1935. The quality and the unfailing technical excellence of these banknotes gave such a stability to the issue that throughout those years the bank simply reprinted the same issue over and over again and, moreover, was able to keep a satisfactory reserve of notes on hand to meet any unexpected requirement.

Although there was no watermark (for the first time since 1884), this issue was of high technical quality and very beautiful, with rich intaglio printing on the front and back – a technique that, with very few exceptions, eventually came to dominate Spanish banknotes. Following tradition, the Cashier's signature was still stamped in the bank's workshop, whereas those of the Governor and Controller were printed in intaglio.

1,000-peseta note of 1907, front

1,000-peseta note of 1907, details of back

After the Second Republic was proclaimed on 14 April 1931 the Government ordered a new issue, commemorating the poet José Zorrilla, from Bradbury Wilkinson. The design of the 1,000-peseta note is not revolutionary, but the security of the note has been noticeably improved, as it is printed in a range of colours in both intaglio and lithography, on watermarked paper.

1,000-peseta note of 1931

500-peseta note of 1936, front

After the Civil War broke out on 18 July 1936, the Burgos Government decided to issue its own banknotes. It failed to agree terms with the firms that had printed banknotes for the Republic (Thomas de la Rue and Bradbury Wilkinson), and commissioned the Leipzig firm of Giesecke & Devrient to manufacture banknotes of 1,000, 500, 100, 50 and 25 pesetas. To save both money and time, these notes were printed by letterpress and lithography. Their most noticeable feature was the paper: the watermark was composed of geometric patterns, and the front of the note carried coloured paper strips printed with the words "Banco de España".

Detail of back: Salamanca Cathedral

Banknotes since the Civil War

The end of the Civil War, followed a little later by the outbreak of World War II, at last offered the bank's directors a longed-for opportunity to nationalise banknote manufacture. After experimenting with a few Spanish and foreign companies, the bank finally entrusted the National Currency and Stamp Works with the task of "ensuring on a permanent basis the manufacture and printing of the banknotes of the Bank of Issue", under a Ministry of Finance decree of 5 April 1940, and since then the Works has manufactured all Spanish banknotes.

1,000-pesta note of 1957, front

Outstanding among all the banknotes issued over the last fifty years is the note dated 29 November 1957 commemorating the Catholic Monarchs Ferdinand and Isabella, and carrying a beautifully engraved double portrait of the crowned and bejewelled king and queen. This note was printed mainly in intaglio on both sides, with very ornate borders. The paper, watermarked with the heads of the royal couple, was made by the National Currency and Stamp Works in its Burgos factory; the company still kept up its old tradition of stamping the Cashier's signature on the note at the bank.

In 1978, the Executive Council of the Bank decided to produce a new banknote series which would use a more up-to-date design together with advanced technical features that would make forgery more difficult. All the denominations of the current series (200, 500, 1,000, 2,000, 5,000 and 10,000 pesetas) carry not only traditional security characteristics, such as intaglio-printed portraits, multicolour backgrounds and watermarked paper, but novel ones as well: paper containing both a plastic security thread and fibres that can be seen only under ultraviolet light, fluorescent intaglio inks and a small motif that can be used to check for perfect register between front and back.

Moreover, the bank has cracked the problems surrounding the automatic machine sorting of notes by including certain secret features on the new notes. These allow special detectors to check, even at high speed, whether a banknote is genuine and to register its denomination. These banknotes are certainly, technically speaking, the most advanced banknotes ever issued by the Bank of Spain.

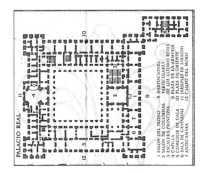

5,000-peseta note of 1978,
details of back

5,000-peseta note of 1978, front

HIGHLIGHTS OF SPANISH BANKNOTE DESIGN

The Banco de San Carlos, Banco de San Fernando and Banco de Isabel II (1782–1856)

Detail from 600-peso banknote of 1797

In 1779, following the war against England, the Spanish Government found itself short of money. A proposal from a group of foreign bankers headed by the Count of Cabarrús seemed to offer a solution; as a result, in September of the following year, the Government launched an issue of royal notes that was the first official paper money circulated in Spain. These royal notes were regarded as both government bonds (with a 20-year maturity period and a 4% interest rate) and paper money. They could be used to pay taxes, were endorsable and were accepted as cash in trading operations; they were not considered as fiduciary currency, however, since they were not allowed to be used to pay wages and pensions, nor were farmers, craftsmen and shopkeepers obliged to accept them. Their face value of 600 pesos (15 times the value of the highest-denomination coin circulating at the time) prevented them from displacing gold and silver.

This first issue was followed a year later by a second, the face value of which was 300 pesos. This led to a depreciation of the currency and as a result (after several unsuccessful attempts) the proposal to set up a National Bank that would gather in all the royal notes in circulation was welcomed by the Count of Floridablanca.

The first Spanish banknotes, called *cédulas*, were issued by the new Banco Nacional de San Carlos on 1 March 1783; their face values ranged from 200 to 1,000 reales. The bank advertised the issue in every way it could think of and tried to explain its purpose to the public – even organising a competition with a cash prize of 6,000 reales for the person who could best demonstrate the notes' usefulness. Each issue of notes was called a series, thus establishing the use of the terms "series" and "denomination" when applied to banknotes that has persisted down to the present day.

The first page of the Banco Nacional de San Carlos' minute book, now kept in the Executive Council Hall of the Bank of Spain, is reproduced opposite.

1759	*Accession of Charles III.*
1778	*Major Spanish ports allowed freedom of trade with America.*
1779	*Spain opposes England in the American War of Independence.*
1780	*First issue of royal bills (paper money used to finance national debt).*
1782	*Creation of the Banco Nacional de San Carlos.*
1783	*Peace of Versailles.*
1788	*Death of Charles III; accession of Charles IV.*
1793	*Spain goes to war against the National Convention Government in France.*
1795	*Peace of Basle.*
1796	*Treaty of San Ildefonso between the Spanish Crown and the French Directoire. War against England.*
1800	*New treaty of San Ildefonso between the Spanish Crown and the French Consulate.*

LIBRO PRIMERO

De Acuerdos reservados de las Juntas y particulares de la Dirección del Banco Nacional de SAN CARLOS, creado por S. M. el Rey nuestro Señor DON CARLOS TERCERO en Real Cedula de 2 de Junio de el Año = 1782

Guilaxte à Salano ba faciebat 1783.

Page from the minute book of the Banco Nacional de San Carlos

The Banco Nacional de San Carlos was liquidated in 1829, and was succeeded by the Banco de San Fernando. In principle, the new bank had a right of issue (limited to Madrid) without any restrictions on amount, although the Government had to authorise each new issue. The denominations of its first issue ranged from 500 to 4,000 reales.

The first banknote, printed on yellow paper in the Engraving Section of the Royal Mint, was technically very simple: the front was printed in black intaglio, with the words "death penalty to forgers" in the border, and the the back was left plain. Banknotes issued after 1843 included some extra security features: four different "blind" (embossed) stamps, a handwritten signature and initials, and hand-cut edges. The borders were intaglio-printed, and become much more complex, including various decorative symbols such as a cock, a dog, a key and a lamp, as well as allegories of commerce, industry and agriculture.

The Banco de San Fernando proved to be too cautious in its issuing policy for the taste of the Minister of Finance, José de Salamanca, who was anxious to make paper money more popular, and with his approval the

Banco de Isabel II was set up in 1844. Since the Banco de San Fernando retained the exclusive privilege of issue, the new bank's notes, which it issued immediately, had to be "bearer notes". Their face values were 200, 500, 1,000, 5,000 and 10,000 reales.

Legislation following the economic crisis of 1847–49, severely restricted the number of notes in circulation. Irked by the limitations set on its activities the Banco de San Fernando, headed by Ramón de Santillán, repeatedly pressed the Government for some easing of the conditions, and at the same time did its best to get its privilege of note issue extended to the whole country.

1801	Peace of Amiens with England.
1804	War against England.
1805	Battle of Trafalgar.
1808	Charles IV abdicates; accession of Ferdinand VII. French troops invade Spain. War of Independence. Ferdinand VII is forced out of Spain and Joseph Bonaparte is enthroned.
1812	The first Constitution is promulgated in Cádiz by the resistance fighters opposing Napoleon.
1814	The French army abandons Spain. Ferdinand VII returns. The absolutist regime is restored.
1820	Liberal revolution.
1823	French intervention in Spain. The absolutist regime is restored again.
1825	Independence of Spanish-American territories, except Cuba and Puerto Rico.
1829	The Banco de San Carlos is liquidated and the Banco de San Fernando is founded. The Commercial Code is enacted.
1831	Foundation of the Madrid Stock Exchange.
1833	Death of Ferdinand VII; accession of Isabella II. Regency of her mother, Queen Maria Cristina. Civil war between the Liberals (Isabella's supporters) and the Traditionalists (supporters of her brother, Prince Charles). Promulgation of Royal Charter (a constitutional charter granted by the Crown).
1835	Minister Mendizábal decrees the public sale of Church properties; the proceeds are used to alleviate the National Debt.
1837	A new Constitution is promulgated, modelled on the Constitution of 1812.
1839	Agreement of Vergara between the Liberal Government and the Traditionalist rebels.
1840	Maria Cristina ceases to be Queen Regent. Government of the Liberal General Espartero.

EL BANCO ESPAÑOL DE S. FERNANDO

Banknote for 1,000 reales de vellon, issued in 1843 by the Banco de San Fernando

The Bank of Spain (1856–1874)

New legislation in 1856 allowed banks throughout the country to issue their own notes; thus although the Banco de San Fernando (which had merged with the Banco de Isabel II in 1847) had rechristened itself the Bank of Spain, it was actually only a Bank of Madrid – as Santillán complained. A ceiling was set to the volume of banknotes issued – three times the bank's real capital plus cash total; the maximum face value of the notes was set at 4,000 reales and the minimum at 100 reales.

Issuing banks sprang up all over the provinces – the total soon reached 21. Their assets varied widely; nevertheless, although Santillán was right to press for a single bank of issue, these provincial banks did a good deal to extend the use of paper money.

Watermark for the 1856 banknote for 1,000 reales de vellon

1843	*Isabella II comes of age. Conservative Government of General Narváez.*
1844	*Banco de Barcelona founded. In addition to the Banco de San Fernando, the Banco de Isabel II is founded in Madrid and is authorised to issue banknotes.*
1845	*New Constitution, similar to the 1834 Royal Charter which limited the powers of the Parliament. Tax reform increases the State's financial capacity.*
1847	*New civil war between the Queen's Government and the Traditionalists. Merger of the Banco de San Fernando and the Banco de Isabel II.*
1849	*The war ends with the defeat of the Traditionalists (the Carlistas).*
1851	*Narváez resigns. New Conservative Government of Bravo Murillo. Public debt reform rejected by foreign creditors.*
1854	*Liberal military uprising. Government of Espartero.*
1855	*General Railway Act. The Minister of Finance, Madoz, decrees the public sale of local authority properties. Foreign investments in Spain begin to rise.*

Bank of Spain note for 1,000 reales de vellon, issued in 1856, front

Bank of Spain note for 200 reales de vellon, issued in 1862, front

A law of 26th June 1864, reformed the monetary system: the new unit of currency was the escudo (equivalent to ten reales), and the divisional units were the peseta (four reales) and the real. By 1871 the value of banknotes circulating in Madrid alone had reached 320 million reales, and large numbers of notes issued by local banks were circulating in the provinces as well.

Banknote for 1,000 reales de vellon, issued by the local bank Banco de Bilbao in 1870

The sole bank of issue (1874–1936)

In 1874 Santillán's dream came true: the Bank of Spain became the country's only bank of issue. It proved a mammoth task to gather in all the provincial banks' notes still in circulation (two of these notes are shown here) and to prevent the issue of bonds or deposit certificates that could be used as paper money. It was not until 1888 that the bank could be sure that the only banknotes circulating in the country were its own – indeed, a few bearer bonds remained in circulation for many years.

1856	*The Banco de San Fernando is renamed the Banco de España. Plurality of banks of issue in provinces is authorised by law. Narváez returns to the Government.*
1857	*Moderate Liberal Government of General O'Donnell.*
1859	*War of Morocco.*
1863	*O'Donnell resigns. International economic crisis.*
1868	*Revolution. Isabella II is deposed. The peseta becomes the official currency, equivalent to the French franc and the Italian lira. Insurrection in Cuba.*
1869	*New Constitution. Free-trade policy.*
1870	*The revolutionary Liberal Government proposes to give the crown to a king of the Savoy dynasty. Prince Amadeus is enthroned as Amadeus I.*
1873	*Proclamation of the First Republic. Draft federalist Constitution not approved. Third civil war between Traditionalists and the Government of Madrid.*
1874	*The Bank of Spain obtains the monopoly of banknote issue. Coup of General Pavia. The Parliament is closed. Isabella II's son is proclaimed King of Spain under the name of Alfonso XII.*

400-escudo note of 1871

Five-peso note issued by the local bank Banco de Barcelona in 1868

The Echegaray's decree of 19 March 1874 that gave the bank the privilege of being the only issuing body in the country also required it to print on its banknotes the name of the branch to which the notes belonged. This local circulation was followed by a regional circulation and the bank attained national circulation by 1884, with 47 branches around the country. As a result the volume of Bank of Spain banknotes in circulation soared, from about 80 million pesetas before 1874 to around 700 million pesetas in 1888; in 1891 a ceiling was set on the amount of paper circulating in the country but this was subsequently raised, and by 1900 the total had climbed to 1,500 million pesetas. Growth continued, until more than 4 billion pesetas were in circulation in 1920 and 5 billion in 1931. From 1898, the amount of notes in circulation was independent of the amount of the bank's capital, although they were still required to be covered by gold.

The banknote illustrated opposite was made by the Bank of Spain itself from an original design by José Villegas and engraved by Bartolomé Maura. The paper contained silk fibres of various colours, and a good watermark. Maura's engraving was poor, however, and Villegas' design did not include a portrait. These shortcomings encouraged forgeries, and the bank soon changed its printing policy.

1876	End of the civil war. Constitution agreed between Conservatives, led by Canovas, and moderate Republicans and Liberals, represented by Sagasta.
1878	End of the Cuban insurrection which started in 1868.
1880	Slavery abolished in West Indies.
1881	Public debt reform implemented by the Minister of Finance, Francisco Camacho.
1882	International financial crisis.
1883	Suspension of banknote convertibility into gold.
1885	Death of Alfonso XII. Regency of his widow, Queen Maria Cristina.
1886	Alfonso XII's posthumous son is born and is immediately proclaimed king under the name of Alfonso XIII.
1889	Enactment of new Civil Code.
1891	Protectionist customs legislation.
1895	Cuban insurrection.
1896	Philippine insurrection.
1897	Murder of Cánovas.
1898	War against the United States. Loss of Cuba, Puerto Rico and the Philippines.
1900	Reorganisation of fiscal and financial system with the aim of stabilisation.
1902	Alfonso XIII comes of age.
1906	The protectionist customs legislation is reaffirmed.

500-peseta note of 1903: details from back (above) and front (below)

One of the handsomest of Spanish banknotes, with beautiful engravings by Enrique Vaquer on both front and back, was in fact never issued. This was the 1,000-peseta note dated 23 May 1915 (shown opposite), which commemorated the visit to the Bank of Spain of King Alfonso XIII and Queen Victoria Eugenia.

Eighteen years on, with the setting up of the Republic on 14 April 1931, everything changed. Most of the 100 million banknotes circulating in Spain were engraved with the likenesses of kings – the 50-peseta note even bore the portrait of the recently deposed Alfonso XIII. The Governor of the Bank of Spain was given the job of adapting the monarchy's banknotes as quickly and safely as possible. The chosen method was to use several different overstampings, but unfortunately the stampings almost disappeared with use. In practice, the public took no notice of the stamps and were ready to accept all sorts of banknotes, whether stamped or not.

The bank was, however, concerned at the loss of five 25-peseta banknotes during production in Bradbury Wilkinson's workshops, and did not wish to become dependent on a single supplier; it therefore ordered a new issue dated 7 January 1935 from Thomas de la Rue. The front of this banknote is rather like that of the Bradbury Wilkinson note, although it is perhaps not of quite such a high quality.

1,000-peseta note of 1915, detail from back

1909	*War in Morocco.*
1910	*Liberal Government of Canalejas.*
1912	*French and Spanish Protectorate over Morocco. Canalejas, head of the Liberal Government, is murdered.*
1914	*Revolutionary political and social agitation. Coalition Government of Liberals, Conservatives and Regionalists.*
1921	*Dato, head of the Conservative Government, is murdered. Aggravation of war in Morocco.*
1923	*Coup d'état of General Primo de Rivera who establishes a dictatorship. The Constitution is abolished and the parliamentary system is suspended.*
1926	*Spanish troops land in Alhucemas; end of war in Morocco. Primo de Rivera replaces the military government with a civilian one.*
1928	*The possibility of reincorporating the gold standard into the Spanish monetary system is studied and rejected.*
1929	*International economic crisis.*
1930	*General Primo de Rivera leaves power.*
1931	*Republican candidates win municipal elections. The Second Republic is proclaimed. King Alfonso XIII leaves Spain.*
1932	*Land Reform Act.*
1933	*Elections won by centre right parties.*
1934	*Revolutionary uprising in Asturias.*

1,000-peseta note of 1915, front

Portrait of King Alfonso XIII, overprinted "República Española"

50-peseta note of 1935, front

The Civil War (1936–39)

The Government of the Republic

The Civil War brought inflation to Spain. The value of paper money in circulation rocketed, from 5,399 billion pesetas on 30 June 1936 across the whole country, to 12,754 billion at the end of the war – through this huge figure referred to notes circulating in the Republican areas only, and did not include lower-denomination notes.

The new Republican issues were originally entrusted partly to Thomas de la Rue and partly to Bradbury Wilkinson, who printed the first 5,000 peseta note in the history of Spain (although it was never circulated). Designed in honour of the painter Fortuny, it was dated Barcelona, 11 June 1938; the front combined a fine intaglio-printed portrait of Fortuny with three-colour offset printing, which was a considerable technical achievement, while the back bore a beautiful reproduction of Fortuny's painting "La Vicaria".

The National Government

The Nationalist Burgos Government, however, failed to reach an agreement with Thomas de la Rue and Bradbury Wilkinson, and commissioned the Leipzig firm of Giesecke & Devrient to produce its 1936 banknotes of 1,000, 500, 50 and 25 pesetas.

Later on, the Burgos Government ordered a new issue from the Milan firm of Coen e Cartevalori, but this issue met with serious supply problems, and a further order was placed with Giesecke & Devrient to print banknotes similar to the old ones.

Issues by other bodies

Meanwhile, the country was experiencing an acute shortage of divisional coins. The nationwide scarcity was due mainly to the catastrophic fall in the value of money under the rule of the Madrid authorities. The hoarding of silver and the debasement of the coinage metal were made up for by huge amounts of paper money. All sorts of bodies began to issue notes – not only regional authorities, but town councils, military units, trade unions, businesses and even private individuals.

The chaos became intolerable, and by a Ministry of Finance decree of 6 January 1938 all the paper money issued by local bodies and institutions was withdrawn. In order to fill the gap left by this money, a new decree passed on 24 February regulated the minting of divisional coins. The circulation of revenue stamps of values 0.10, 0.25 and 0.50 pesetas was provisionally authorised. They were stuck to 35-mm cardboard discs manufactured by the National Currency and Stamp Works, with crossed fibres (difficult to imitate) and Spain's coat of arms with a mural crown printed on one face.

1936	*Elections won by Popular Front. Army rebellion in Morocco. The Civil War begins.*
1939	*General Franco wins the Civil War and proclaims the end of the Republic.*

5,000-peseta note of 1938, front and back

From 1939 to the present day

The huge monetary problems that faced Spain at the end of the Civil War were tackled with the Unblocking Law of 7 December 1939 (introduced by Larraz), through which payments returned to normal in the country and a base was laid to reconstruct the Bank of Spain and repair the war-damaged currency. Under the Laws of 9 November 1939, the Bank of Spain's notes had already been declared full legal tender, with the resulting suspension of the metal guarantee system for which the Banking Law of 1929 had provided.

As a further step, under the Law of 13 March 1942, the balance-sheets of the Bank of Spain, hitherto presented separately for the two zones of the country, were merged into a single document in a form that corresponded to the bank's operational system. It was now essential to reduce liabilities, among which the largest was 12,754 billion pesetas' worth of "red" banknotes; these had to be matched by the Bank of Spain through issues ordered in Italy and Germany during the Civil War and in early 1940.

World War II increased the difficulties in obtaining foreign supplies and led the bank (after an unsuccessful attempt to create a mint with private capital) to place its orders exclusively with the National Currency and Stamp Works, although on 24 June 1941 it was authorised to use suppliers if there was a special need.

The factory was overwhelmed with work from the very beginning. As well as responding to the coin scarcity by producing vast numbers of divisional banknotes (denominations lower than 25 pesetas), it had also to meet the requirements of a circulation that, in 1941, had already reached 127.4 million banknotes (in denominations of 25 and 1,000 pesetas) and 12.893 billion pesetas.

To ease the immediate pressure on the Mint, the first post-Civil War banknotes were printed by the Italian firm Calcografia e Cartevalori (the successor to Coen e Cartevalori). The 500-peseta note was the best of this series, which included notes for 25, 50, 100, 500 and 1,000 pesetas, although only the last two values were printed in intaglio.

*50-peseta note of 1940, detail from back showing a scene
from the "Battle of Lepanto"*

By March 1940, however, the Works was able to sign a contract for the production of the issue of 500- and 1,000-peseta notes dated 21 October 1940, and since then every Spanish banknote has been printed there; moreover, since 1953 it has manufactured all its banknote paper at its Burgos plant.

One of its finest banknotes of recent years is the 1000-peseta note of 1971, designed to honour the Spanish Minister of Finance and Nobel prizewinner of 1904, José Echegaray, and issued to commemorate the Bank of Spain's first hundred years as the sole bank of issue.

1947	*Succession Law provides for a Monarchy to succeed General Franco.*
1953	*Defence agreements between Spain and the United States.*

500-peseta note of 1940, front

1,000-peseta note of 1971, front

The Bank of Spain building

The current series of Spanish banknotes was designed in 1978 and issued from 1982 onwards; the back of the 10,000-peseta note shows a portrait of the young crown prince, Felipe de Borbón, with a view of El Escorial Monastery in the backround.

1955	*Spain joins the United Nations.*
1959	*Stabilisation plan, ending the autocratic system in force in the Spanish economy since the end of the Civil War.*
1964	*First Economic and Social Development Plan.*
1969	*Juan Carlos de Borbón, grandson of Alfonso XIII, proclaimed heir to the Crown.*
1975	*General Franco dies. Prince Juan Carlos accedes to the throne under the name of Juan Carlos I.*
1977	*First democratic parliamentary elections in more than fifty years.*
1978	*New Constitution confirms the parliamentary monarchy regime.*
1984	*Spain joins the European Economic Community.*

10,000-peseta note of 1985, back

Numero Sexton Tuß: Fembtij

Nº 16599

At thenne Creditif- Zedels Jnnehafwande ha
Banco sub Nº 16599 — at fordra Tiugu Fe
mynt thet warder aff oß vnderteknade Banco C
hållare attesterat; Såsom ock medh thet ther t
Sigillet verificerat. Dat. Stokholms Banco Ar

Daler 25. Kopparmynt.

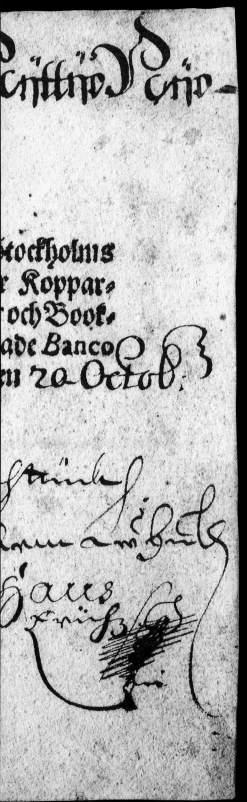

SWEDEN

HINC ROBUR ET SECURITAS.

Banknote of 1663

In the middle of the seventeenth century, the Swedish economy ran into serious trouble. For a long time copper plaques had been used as a means of payment – they were probably the most absurdly heavy and unwieldy coins in the world, the largest weighing around 20 kg. Because of a depreciation of the currency in 1660 the metal value of the copper plaques came to exceed their face value, and following Gresham's law ("bad money drives out good") they disappeared. A decision was taken to make lighter coins, but it was not possible to issue enough of them to cover demand.

Clearly there was an urgent need for an alternative method of payment.

The first banknotes

Such a method had already been recommended in 1652 by Johan Palmstruch, a Dutchman from Riga. The government gave him permission to found the first Swedish bank, Stockholms Banco (the Stockholm Bank) and on 16 July, 1661 the new bank issued notes of credit (*kreditivsedler*), whose value depended upon the level of public confidence in the bank.

Seal embossed on a 1663 note

Copper "coin" of 1644

Johan Palmstruch's signature

The new notes of credit were the first banknotes, not only in Sweden but anywhere in Europe. Some earlier certificates issued by Italian banks had some of the qualities of banknotes, but those of the Stockholm Bank were different in several important aspects. First, they were not issued against cash deposits in the bank. Secondly, their amounts were in round figures, which were printed on the notes. Thirdly, they were not issued to a specified person but were valid in the hands of the bearer without endorsement and finally, they attracted no interest.

The Swedish economist and historian Professor Eli F. Heckscher has pointed out Palmstruch's claim to a place in the history of money and banking as the inventor of the banknote. He adds that the promissory notes introduced later in the same century by Scottish and English banks were of the same character and influenced future developments infinitely more – but, he argues, Palmstruch's notes were their forerunner. Most modern economists and historians accept Heckscher's view, but lively debate still surrounds the rival claims of the paper currency issued in China in the Middle Ages. These were strictly government notes and not banknotes however, and their issue does not seem to have had any influence on the use of paper money in Europe.

The 1661 notes of credit were very well received by tradesmen and merchants, who even praised God for the provision of convenient banknotes in place of the heavy copper money.

These first banknotes were printed by letterpress. The numbers of the notes, in letters and figures were handwritten on the front and the back; the date of issue was also handwritten. Palmstruch and four of the bank's employees wrote their signatures on each note below the printed text, and the Stockholm Bank's large seal was embossed on a square piece of paper fixed by a wafer to the front of the note. The banknote paper did not carry any specific watermark; the printer was probably authorised to use any kind of paper available.

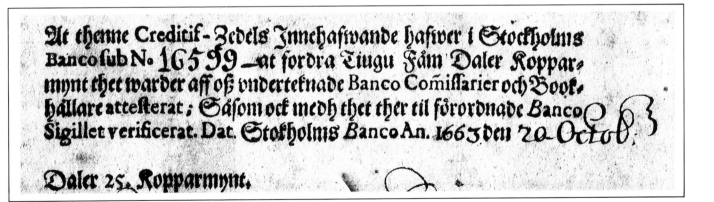

25-daler note of 1663 (detail) – notes were still denominated in copper currency

No note from 1661 is extant but some banknotes issued in 1662 and 1663 still survive in various museums.

The Stockholm Bank handled the new invention very cautiously at first, but in 1663 it began to grant a great many loans which were repaid in notes of credit. The result was inevitable: the bank had to announce that it was unable to redeem the notes or to honour cheques drawn by the public.

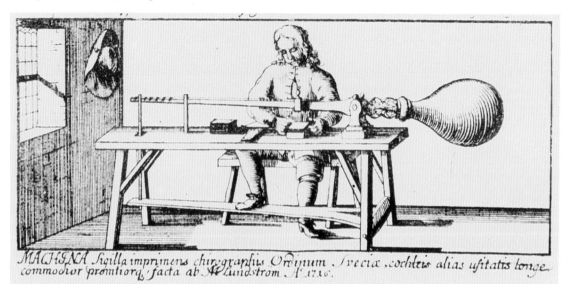

*Die-stamping press
(a print made in 1716)*

The first security features

In 1665, the Government decided that notes of credit denominated in copper money should be converted into notes denominated in silver, and so the "copper-money" currency had to be abolished. Although the Government had decided not to issue any more banknotes, notes of credit were issued in 1666.

The existing notes had been extensively forged, and in response the bank deliberately set out to produce new notes of a quality high enough to frustrate the counterfeiters. Three new security features were introduced.

1658	*The second Danish war starts. The author Georg Stiernhielm publishes* Hercules, *the first epic volume in Swedish.*
1660	*The war with Denmark ends; with Sweden ceding the province of Trondheim and the island of Bornholm to Denmark.*
	A regency is set up for the young King Karl XI.
1662	*The Queen Mother, Hedvig Eleonora, starts building the Royal Castle at Drottningholm; the architect is Nikodemus Tessin the Elder.*
1663	*Collegium Medicum (the first Medical Board) is founded.*
1668	*Treaty between Sweden, Holland and the United Kingdom against France. The Swedish Central Bank, Sveriges Rikes Standers Bank (later the Bank of Sweden) is founded. The University of Lund opens.*

The first was the use of watermarked paper, containing a watermark specifically designed for the purpose in which the word BANCO clearly appears – these banknotes may have been the first to use a purpose-made watermark. From the bank records of the time, it appears that the paper was manufactured at a private paper mill near Stockholm.

The second new security feature was die stamping. The notes carried eight signatures, and each signatory's personal seal was die-stamped on the note; three different seals of the Stockholm Bank, all of different sizes, were also stamped on the face. The die stamping was all carried out in the Royal Mint, which had suitable equipment for the purpose.

Die stamps on banknotes

Finally, the quality of the ornamentation marked out the 1666 issue. The banknotes were given a decorative border, made up from elements available in the composing room – a style of ornamentation thought to present a problem to the would-be counterfeiter.

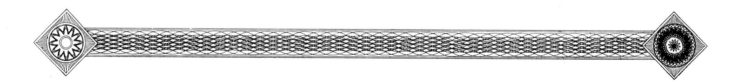

All the 1666 notes of credit were printed from two plates, and the same printing press seems to have been used for all denominations by changing the plates. The two plates can be distinguished by the slightly different shapes of the decorative frames and by variations in typeface and in the spelling of some of the words in the text.

The printer's name is not known; at that time, however, only three printers were operating in Stockholm and only one of them, Ignatius Meurer, is mentioned in the Stockholm Bank's records; probably, therefore, the notes were produced in Meurer's works.

During 1667 the bank issued a new type of banknote: the transfer note, a document given to a person who had deposits on the transfer account in the bank. These notes circulated as banknotes and were signed by both parties on transfer. Often personal wax seals were used as well, as shown in the illustration on page 272.

100-daler note of 1666,
front and back, and personal seals
— notes were now denominated
in silver currency

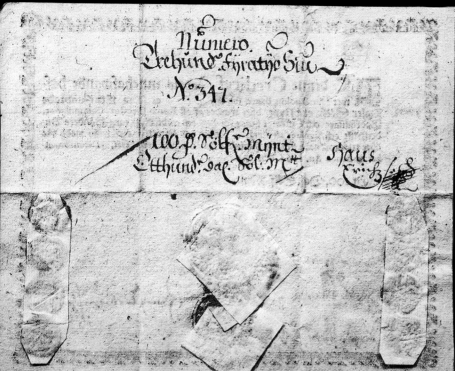

The Bank of Sweden is born

In 1668, the Swedish Parliament founded a new bank, the Rikets Ständers Bank (Bank of the Estates of the Realm) the predecessor of the Sveriges Riksbank (Bank of Sweden).

Unlike all other banks, this bank was controlled directly by Parliament, and was not allowed to issue notes of credit or similar notes. The bank stuck to the rules for the first three decades of its life, but in the meantime the public became more and more accustomed to using substitutes for banknotes – approved cheques, deposit receipts and payment orders, for instance.

In 1701, the Parliamentary Banking Committee issued a notice "Introducing a new means of payment", the "new means" was called the transfer note. Both the original idea and the name were probably borrowed from the Stockholm Bank's transfer notes issued in 1667. The new transfer note remained in use for 140 years, with only minor changes; some are illustrated on the next few pages together with those details that altered during their long life.

In 1729 in order to make the notes more difficult to counterfeit, the board of directors of the bank introduced die-stamped paper, made by a process very like that of striking a coin, and in the same year they added a die-stamped medallion showing a seated woman usually nicknamed Svea, who symbolised Sweden.

Gradually the procedure for the transfer of notes fell into disuse; the endorsement procedure had become impractical as soon as low-denomination notes began to be used by illiterate people. The bank started to issue banknotes without any endorsement requirements, carrying the wording: "This banknote is valid in the hands of the bearer".

Die stamping on the transfer note of 1748

Numero Sectton

At *Sr Abraham Momma* ———————
eller den hwilken han denne sub N° 15: Transport-Zedel medh egen Hand
vnderskrifwit och Signetes förseglande warder transporterandes; Vthi detta
Stockholmiske Banco hafwer at fordra Ett hundrade Dal. Sölf. Mynt. vthi
Kopparpenningar blifwer här medh aff oss vnderteknade Banco Commissarier
och Bookhållare attesterat; Såsom och medh thet ther til förordnade Banco Sigillet verificerat. Datum Stockholms Banco den 14: octobris A.° 1667 ———

100. Daler Sölfwermynt vthi Kopparpenningar.

Desse bem." Ett hundrade Dal. Sölf. Mynt warda transporteradhe
ifrån migh *Abraham Momma* til *Sr Henric Classen*
————— Datum Stockholm 15 octob. 1667

Desse bem." Ett hundrade Dal. Sölf. Mynt warda transporteradhe
ifrån migh *Lars Classon* —— til *Iwer Claudes*
Hagersticina —— Datum Stockholm 16 octob. 1667

Desse bem." Ett hundrade Dal. Sölf. Mynt warda transporteradhe
ifrån migh *Claude Hagersbierna* til *Sr Lorentz Alba-*
nus ————— Datum Stockholm 19 octob. 1667

Desse bem." Ett hundrade Dal. Sölf. Mynt warda transporteradhe
ifrån migh *Lorentz Albanus* til *Alexander Magillud*
—— 11 Datum Stockholm 19 octob. 1667

Desse bem." Ett hundrade Dal. Sölf. Mynt warda transporteradhe
ifrån migh *Alexander pattillock* til *monsr Petter Selfing*
————— Datum Stockholm 21 octob. a° 1667

Desse bem." Ett hundrade Dal. Sölf. Mynt warda transporteradhe
ifrån migh *Petter Söfing* til *Banco*
Datum Stockholm 21 octob. A° 1667

(second sheet, partially visible)

Desse bem." Ett hundrade Dal. Sölf. Mynt warda transporteradhe
... til *Biron*
Datum ... A° 1667

Desse bem." Ett hundrade Dal. Sölf. Mynt warda transporteradhe
... til *Sr ... Stockholm* 67

... Ett hundrade Dal. Sölf. Mynt warda transporteradhe
... *George Christoff Poty* til *Henric Berman*
Datum 14 novemb. ibby in Stockholm

... Ett hundrade Dal. Sölf. Mynt warda transporteradhe
... *Hinrich Bohman* til *Banco*
Datum 12 December A° 1667

Ett hundrade Dal. Sölf. Mynt warda transporteradhe
... R. Banco til *Mons: Jean Jürst*
Datum 23 Jan. 1668

... hundrade Dal. Sölf. Mynt warda transporteradhe
Jean Jürst —— til *Banco*
Datum Stockh. 1668 vrfed

... hundrade Dal. Sölf. Mynt warda transporteradhe
————— til
Datum

... hundrade Dal. Sölf. Mynt warda transporteradhe
————— til
Datum

... Dal. Sölf. Mynt warda transporteradhe
————— til
Datum

... Dal. Sölf. Mynt warda transporteradhe
til
Datum

Legal tender

In 1745, paper money became the official Swedish currency. Every citizen was obliged to accept the notes, and the need for endorsement was finally abolished. Banknotes had come of age, and were now legal tender in the full sense.

The Bank takes over

In 1747, the Parliamentary Banking Committee decided to use special founts of type for the text on banknotes. A typesetter was employed, and given a workshop in the bank's premises in the old town of Stockholm. The same year, the Committee decided that the banknotes should be printed at the bank rather than at a private printing works, and also transferred the die stamping of the notes from the Royal Mint to the bank building. The building has appeared on the bank's medal ever since 1729, as well as on the ten-kronor banknote since 1968 and the new 500-kronor banknote since 1985.

In 1748, the denominations on the banknotes began to be printed in Finnish as well as in Swedish.

Transfer note of 1748 with denomination in Finnish

The Bank of Sweden building on the bank's medal of 1729

N:o 1748

SVERIGES RIKES STÄNDERS
BANCO TRANSPORT SEDEL

Banco-Transport-Sedel N:o 35003

Uti Riksens Ständers Wäxel-Banco hafwer Banco-
Commissarien H:r Johan A. Keintin

insatt på Transport-Räkningen Trettio Sex Daler
K:mt. hwilka 36 Daler K:mt böra egenhändigt och tyde-
ligen transporteras med dag och åhre-tahl, ifrån man
till man; Skolandes innehafwaren af then sidsta trans-
porten utbekomma ofwan bemälte Summa.
Stockholm then 5 augusti Anno 1748

Säg Trettio Sex Daler K:mt.

Euus nälj ättå kymmendä
Daleri kupar raha.

In 1754, forged transfer notes were circulating in worryingly large numbers, and the bank decided to improve its security. Within the year it had established its own paper mill at Tumba, not far from Stockholm, and the first banknote paper from the mill was presented to the directors in 1759. This banknote paper was considered to be of fine quality and was watermarked with a pair of cornucopias.

This period was not without its difficulties, however. Between 1701 and 1839, a variety of different monetary units was used, some of them convertible and others not, which caused considerable confusion. Furthermore, the fall in the value of money led to the issue in 1812 of low denomination banknotes that needed no endorsement.

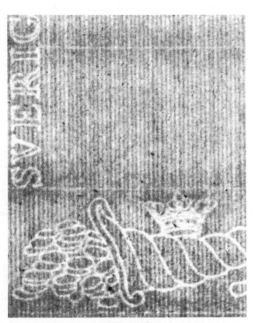

Watermark

Notes denominated in different monetary units

1672	Karl XI comes of age.
1675–79	War between Denmark and Sweden.
1689	Ex-Queen Kristina dies in Rome and is buried in St Peter's Church.
1697	Karl XII is crowned. Coronation of Karl XII. The Royal Castle in Stockholm is destroyed by fire.
1699	Secret treaty against Sweden between Saxony-Poland and Denmark, joined by Tsar Peter of Russia.
1700–18	The Great Nordic war: Sweden loses its Baltic provinces, most of its provinces in Germany and, temporarily, Finland. The 150 year old struggle to dominate the Baltic Sea ends.
1718	King Karl XII is killed (probably murdered) during a campaign at Fredrikshald in Norway.
1719	New constitution, limiting the power of the King.
1720	The Russian Navy raids the Swedish east coast. Peace with Prussia. Fredrick av Hessen is elected King, under the name of Fredrik I.
1721	Peace with Russia.
1726	A Government decree prohibits religious meetings outside the State Church.
1731	The East India Company is established.
1741	Sweden declares war on Russia.
1742	The physicist Anders Celsius publishes his thesis on the Celsius thermometric scale.

Transfer note of 1787

¹⁄₆-Riksdaler coin of 1788,
obverse and reverse

Guilloche pattern by C. A. Broling

Watermark and coloured banknote paper, 1835

The drive for quality

In the early 1830s the bank found itself under fire from critics of its printing methods – all notes were still printed only by letterpress – and of the quality of its banknote paper. The bank decided to investigate paper qualities and printing techniques in other countries, and sent two Swedish scientists to London, Berlin and Paris to collect information about banknote paper and printing; they also sought information about banknote printing in the United States of America.

The next step was the introduction of machine-engraved patterns on the banknotes. Carl Abraham Broling, an engraver at the Royal Mint, had invented a geometric lathe (see page 36) and he was prepared to use this machine to produce a new series of banknotes. This move substantially improved the quality of the designs.

In 1855, a new monetary unit was announced: the Riksdaler Riksmynt divided into 100 equal parts called öre.

The sizes of the notes issued in 1852 and 1861 were related to their values. Of the three notes of the issue, the highest-denomination note was three times the size, and the second highest twice the size, of the lowest-denomination note.

1743	*Peace with Russia. Parts of Finland ceded.*
1749	*A Government office is formed to collect population statistics.*
1750s	*The predominant industries are mining and iron working. Sweden supplies 40% of the world consumption of pig-iron – 75% of her total exports.*
1753	*The Gregorian Calendar is introduced. A new Royal Palace is completed in Stockholm. The scientist Carl von Linné publishes his book* Species Plantarum *on the classification of plants.*
1756	*The European seven year war between Prussia and Saxony begins. Sweden supports Saxony.*

Carl von Linné

Two-Riksdaler note of 1849

Ten-Riksdaler note of 1859

May 1873 saw the introduction of the gold standard, together with another new monetary unit called the krona, which like its predecessor was divided into 100 öre. The new series of banknotes that followed had machine-engraved backgrounds, borders and guilloches, and were printed in more than one colour.

A more elaborately patterned series of kronor notes was issued in 1880 (although it is usually called the 1879 series) but by 1884 counterfeits were already circulating and the manager of the Riksbank's banknote printing works, Jacob Bagge, proposed the immediate production of a new series.

1762	Peace with Prussia.
1763	Jean Baptiste Bernadotte (later King Karl XIV Johan) is born in Pau in France. Economic crisis in Sweden; many industries close down.
1766	The first Swedish law protecting the freedom of the press is passed.
1772	Coronation of Gustav III; a coup d'état restores the power of the Crown. A new constitution is adopted, abolishing torture in prisons.
1776	In a reform of the economy, old banknotes are redeemed in silver at half their face value.
1778	Capital punishment for certain crimes is abolished.
1779	The chemist Jöns Jacob Berzelius is born.
1786	The Swedish Academy is founded by Gustav III.
1789	The Supreme Court is established.
1792	King Gustav III is shot at a masquerade ball at the Opera, and dies two weeks later.
1795	The poet Carl Michael Bellman dies.
1808	War with Russia.
1809	Sweden surrenders Finland to Russia. New constitution (6 June).
1814	A Norwegian constitution is formed (17 May). Karl XIII is King of Sweden and Norway.
1818	Karl XIV Johan is crowned. Jöns Jacob Berzelius is appointed Secretary of the Swedish Academy of Science.
1820	The first Swedish Savings Bank is established in Gothenburg.
1825	The Royal Institute of Technology in Stockholm is founded.
1830	The liberal newspaper Aftonbladet is founded by Lars Johan Hierta.
1831	Skånska Privatbanken, the oldest private bank in Sweden, is established.
1832	The Göta Canal between the North Sea and the Baltic Sea is completed. The first papermaking machine is installed at the Klippan paper mill.
1834	In an attempt to stabilise the monetary system; banknotes are redeemed at half their value.
1842	Regulations are introduced to establish free schools in every parish.
1846	The guild institutions are abolished.
1849	The writer August Strindberg is born.
1855	The Swedish telegraph system is connected to the European network. The first postage stamp is issued.
1856	The first Swedish railway opens.
1858	The Bessemer steelmaking process is introduced. Religious freedom is extended.
1863	Alfred Nobel invents dynamite.
1866	The old Parliament with the system of four Estates votes to reform itself.
1867	The first assembly of the new two chamber Parliament.
1869	Crop failure in Sweden. Emigration to North America increases, with about 40,000 people emigrating every year.

Alfred Nobel

No 089904,D   No 089904,D

Sveriges   **Riksbank**

inlöser, vid anfordran, denna sedel å

Kronor **ETT HUNDRA** **Kronor**

med guldmynt enligt lagen om rikets mynt af den 30 Maj 1873.

Stockholm den 2 Januarii 1877.

100   100   100

100-kronor note of 1877

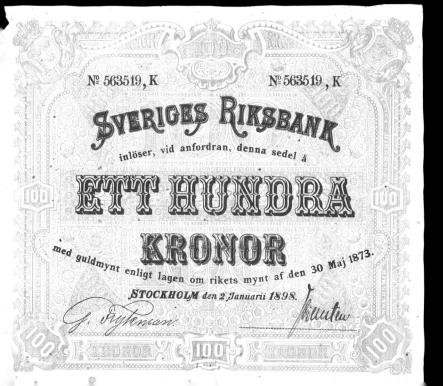

No 563519 , K   No 563519 , K

SVERIGES RIKSBANK

inlöser, vid anfordran, denna sedel å

ETT HUNDRA

KRONOR

med guldmynt enligt lagen om rikets mynt af den 30 Maj 1873.

STOCKHOLM den 2 Januarii 1898.

100   KRONOR   100   KRONOR   100

100-kronor note of 1898

Intaglio printing arrives

Bagge's design for the new notes were ready by the following year, and the series was issued during the 1890s. The backgrounds were printed in colour by letterpress, with plates produced by the stereotype process; the main design, which included a two-colour guilloche on the front, was intaglio-printed. Although this made counterfeiting more difficult, it pushed up production costs – new printing equipment had to be bought, the printing technique was complicated and the engraving of the plates was expensive, the more so as no Swedish engravers were available and the engraving had to be done abroad.

Guilloche with numeral "5"

Five-kronor note of 1890

1876	*L. M. Ericsson sets up a company for the manufacture of telephones.*
1879	*August Strindberg's* The Red Room *is published.*
1880	*A. E. Nordenskiöld returns to Stockholm with his ship Vega after sailing through the North East Passage.*
1891	*The first automobile in Sweden is shown at an exhibition in Gothenburg. Selma Lagerlöf's novel Gösta Berlings Saga is published.*
1892	*The first municipal electricity works opens in Stockholm.*
1895	*The first electric railway in Sweden.*
1897	*The Bank of Sweden is granted the sole right of banknote issue. The explorer Sven Hedin returns from his first expedition to Central Asia.*
1901	*The first Nobel prizes, are awarded.*
1905	*The union between Norway and Sweden is dissolved.*
1907	*King Gustav V succeeds Oskar II.*
1909	*Widespread industrial unrest in Sweden.*
1910	*The guillotine is used in Sweden for the first and only time. Capital punishment is abolished thereafter.*
1912	*The Olympic Games are held in Stockholm.*
1917	*A new Swedish translation of the Bible is approved.*
1919	*Laws are passed about an eight hour working day.*
1920	*Death of the painter Anders Zorn, best known for his paintings of Dalecarlia.*
1923	*The Town Hall in Stockholm is completed.*

100-kronor note of 1918, front

Details from notes of the 1890 series

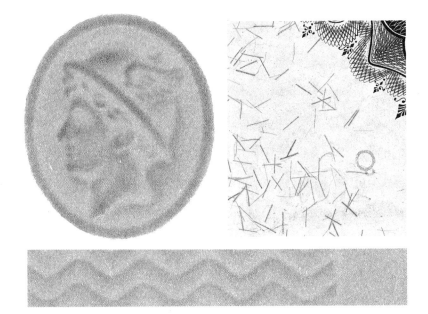

The paper of the 1890 notes was covered with a wavy-line watermark, with a head of Mercury in the lower left-hand corner. The five- and 50-kronor notes were pink with blue fibres embedded in the paper forming a vertical stripe on the back, and the other notes were pale blue with a stripe of red fibres.

Watermarks and coloured fibres in banknote paper

The intaglio print was very delicate; it used a whole range of grey tones, finely engraved portraits, black-and-white line patterns and microlettering. The Gothic style of the bank's name, Sveriges Riksbank, on the front of the note evinced the German influence in the design.

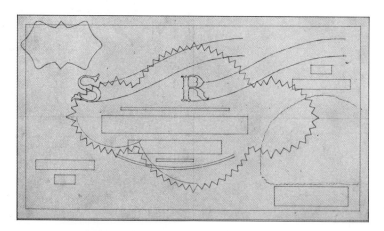

*Layouts for a
ten-kronor note (not used)*

Sketch for Svea motif (not used) *Jkg. 93.*

Some of the drawings made in preparation for the 1890 notes have survived, and are illustrated on pages 284 to 286. Preliminary layout sketches, a figure "5" surrounded by an ornate guilloche and a detail drawing for the 1,000-kronor note give a good idea of the issue. The rough sketches for the allegorical Svea figure were never used, but the much-loved Svea does appear in one form or another not only on these notes but for comparison, the front and back of the ten-kronor note, with some details of the design, are also illustrated.

Some of the notes of the 1890 series remained in use for nearly seventy years. One reason for their long life was the number of their security features – still a significant deterrent to counterfeiters even today, and one for which the designers and printers deserve full credit.

Ten-kronor note of 1892, with Svea on the front and a portrait of King Gustav I (1496—1560) on the back

10,000 kronor notes of 1939 and 1958

Detail from back of
five-kronor note of 1954: Svea

By 1939 a high value banknote was needed, and the 10,000-kronor note was issued. It looked rather like an English pound note, had a full watermark and was printed in two-colour intaglio on one side only. It was replaced by a new 10,000-kronor note in 1958.

In 1941, a new ten-kronor note was issued, followed in 1948 by a commemorative note to celebrate the ninetieth birthday of King Gustav V.

A new 1,000-kronor note was issued in 1952, and a new five-kronor note in 1954, while in 1968 the 300th anniversary of the foundation of the Bank of Sweden was commemorated in a special ten-kronor note.

1925	*The broadcasting of regular radio programmes begins.*
1931	*Archbishop Nathan Söderblom dies. Sweden abandons the gold standard.*
1932	*The Swedish industrial leader Ivar Kreuger commits suicide in Paris.*
1946	*The Scandinavian airline, SAS is formed.*
1955	*Death of the sculptor Carl Milles.*
1961	*Dag Hammarsköld, Secretary General of the United Nations, is killed in an air crash at Ndola in Zambia.*

1000-kronor note of 1952, front

Ten-kronor note of 1947, front and back

Ten-kronor note of 1968 commemorating the Bank of Sweden's tercentenary, front

Detail from back: the Bank of Sweden building

With the invention of the web press in the 1950s, it became possible to produce banknotes in a single process, starting with a reel of unprinted paper and ending with finished sheets of notes. In 1961, the five-kronor note became the first note to be web-printed. Since its launch in 1954 this note had been produced with an accurately positioned watermark, but at the time this positioning could not be achieved with the web press, and the new notes were produced with a a band watermark. This note was also the first Swedish banknote to contain a security thread.

All issues of notes after 1890 were made either in response to a specific need (as, for example, the 10,000-kronor notes) or to commemorate special occasions. The ten-kronor, 1,000-kronor and five-kronor notes issued in 1941, 1952 and 1954 respectively were introduced as the first values for a new series which was never completed.

| 1968 | The tercentenary of the Bank of Sweden: a commemorative banknote is issued. |
| 1985 | Olaf Palme assassinated. |

SVERIGES RIKSBANK

1954

FEM KRONOR

5

5

AA 000001

Five-kronor note of 1954 and 1961, front and back

HINC ROBUR ET SECURITAS

Between 1960 and 1965 another new series of notes was produced in response to a Parliamentary initiative, intended to help visually handicapped people, requiring a different size of note for each denomination. All the old banknote sizes were discarded, and new ones introduced.

The current series of banknotes, made possible by new advanced web-printing techniques, was launched in 1985 with the issue of the 500-kronor note, followed by the 100-kronor note two years later; the next few years will also see a new 1,000-kronor note and a 50-kronor note. The present ten-kronor note is not being redesigned, and will remain in use until it is eventually replaced by a coin.

100-kronor note of 1987, front and back, and detail from front

500-kronor note of 1986, front and back, and detail from back

1965 DZ

A 000000

Five-kronor note of 1965, front and back

N° (110) 20ˢ

THIS Indented Bill of Twenty
Shillings due from the Massachusets
Colony to the Possessor shallbe in value
equal to money & shallbe accordingly
accepted by the Treasurer and Receivers
subordinate to him in all Publick payments
and for any Stock at any time in the
Treasury Boston in New-England
February the third 1690 By Order of
the General Court

Bill for 20 shillings, issued 1690

UNITED STATES OF AMERICA

EARLY BANKNOTES

The first copper printing plates

American banknote history dawned with the printing of bills of credit for the Massachusetts Bay Colony of 1690. Hand-engraved copper plates were used, but these could produce only a limited number of impressions before having to be re-engraved; the bills therefore varied slightly – a defect that proved a 'gift to the colony's counterfeiters. Dubious paper money was less than welcome to the soldiers who were being paid off after the unsuccessful Canadian campaign, and as inflation rose the bills came to be discounted in favour of coins with an intrinsic value.

Innovators

The long list of innovators in banknote printing includes some unexpected names – for example, that of the statesman and scientist Benjamin Franklin, who was apprenticed to a printer at the age of twelve. Never a man to do things by halves, Franklin not only printed notes for the colony of New Jersey in the late 1720s, but built his own press for the purpose, and cut and cast the ornaments that decorated the notes as well.

Paul Revere, too, dabbled in banknote printing; he engraved and printed the notes issue by the Provincial Congress of Massachusetts and New Hampshire in 1775.

1773	*The "Boston Tea Party": tea belonging to the English East India Company is dumped into Boston Harbour by American colonists.*
1774	*The first Continental Congress meets in Philadelphia.*
1776	*Adoption of the Declaration of Independence, which was largely written by Thomas Jefferson.*
1781	*Capitulation of British troops under General Cornwallis at Yorktown.*
1783	*Peace of Paris: Great Britain recognises American independence.*
1787	*The United States Constitution is drafted.*
1792	*Coinage Act establishes the dollar as the monetary unit of the United States.*
1807	*The steamship* Clermont, *designed by Robert Fulton, sails up the Hudson river.*
1812	*War between the United States and Great Britain.*

$2 Federal Reserve note, of 1976, showing the signing of The Declaration of Independence

George Washington, first President of the United States (1789–97)

$1 coin, obverse and reverse

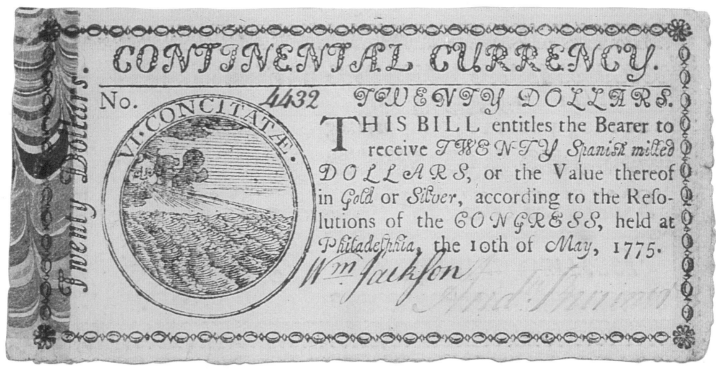

"Continental" note of 1775, for 20 Spanish dollars

"Not worth a Continental"

America's War of Independence against Britain drained the young state of funds, and on 10 May 1775 the Continental Congress decided to issue paper money, payable in Spanish milled dollars. These notes carried a combination of border and emblem cuts, handset type and copperplate engraving and they were soon widely counterfeited.

Within five years these "Continental" notes, once accepted throughout colonial America except in the British-occupied territories, almost completely lost their value. Washington wrote of them that "a whole wagon full of paper money barely suffices to buy a wagon full of food". The phrase "not worth a Continental" as an synonym for complete worthlessness still survives in America today.

"Nature print" by Benjamin Franklin

The "American system"

Jacob Perkins of Newburyport, Massachusetts, came next in the line of pioneer American banknote printers. In 1799 he patented his system for making sheets of intaglio-printed banknotes, and improved it further in 1804.

Perkins used punches to stamp letters and designs on to a soft steel cylinder (a cumbersome process that was later simplified). The cylinder was hardened, and then rolled under pressure on to individual copper plates or dies, so transferring the design it carried. Lettering and the name of the issuing bank were engraved directly on the dies. Four of these dies were assembled in a metal frame, so making a four-subject printing plate. Later, the copper plates were replaced by more durable steel.

The versatile Perkins, a skilled engineer and metallurgist, then turned to developing a reversed version of his transfer process. He took a hardened steel plate carrying an engraved design and rolled a soft cylinder back and forth across it; the cylinder thereupon picked up the design in relief. Once hardened, the cylinder could then transfer the design to as many plates as might be required; these were hardened in their turn, and then were usually assembled into a four-subject printing plate. The system became known as siderography or, sometimes, the "American System". Intaglio plates are still produced today by an improved version of Perkins' process.

An early banknote produced by Perkins' siderographic process

The transformation of the banknote

The invention of siderography revolutionised the appearance of Banknotes. Intricate line patterns and pictorial motifs such as portraits and landscapes replaced the simple ornaments and calligraphy of the early notes; portraits in particular catch the eye, and even a casual observer can easily detect the tiny variations of line that almost inevitably appear in a forgery.

Motifs symbolising
Mechanics and Navigation

A Californian mine
at the time of the "Gold Rush"

1823	*The Monroe Doctrine is formulated.*
1825	*Eli Whitney, inventor of the cotton gin, dies.*
1827	*Establishment of the Baltimore & Ohio Railway, the first railway system in the United States.*
1835	*American humorist Mark Twain (pseudonym of Samuel Langhorne Clemens) is born in Florida, Missouri.*
1839	*Baseball is invented in Cooperstown, New York, by Abner Doubleday.*
1844	*Establishment of the first telegraph line between Washington DC and Baltimore.*
1846	*War between the United States and Mexico.*
1849	*The Great Californian Gold Rush.*
1853	*Matthew C. Perry establishes diplomatic and commercial relations between the United States and Japan.*
1854	*Republican party is founded.*

Chartered banks

The memory of the Continental currency disaster died hard. The first Bank to be chartered was the Bank of North America, on 31 December 1781. Ten years later, two more banks received charters – the Bank of New York and the Providence Bank – but it was the Bank of the United States (1791–1811 and 1816–36) that first created controversy. The first charter of this Bank was allowed to lapse and President Andrew Jackson, who favoured private banks, vetoed a charter of renewal.

Numerous private and state banks continued to issue their own notes, although many of them lacked funds to back their issue. In 1863, following the issue of paper money by the U.S. Treasury two years before, these banks were offered a choice between joining the national banking system and paying a ten per cent tax on notes issued; this forced them into the system as the only alternative to closure.

The first bank (1791–1811) established by Congress upon the urging of Alexander Hamilton

Distinctive paper

In 1869, the Treasury signed a contract with Messrs J. M. Willcox & Cox of Philadelphia for the manufacture of watermarked currency paper carrying conspicuous vertical stripes, two or three inches wide, of dark blue jute fibres embedded in the paper.

Willcox & Cox patented the new paper, and continued to manufacture it for the Government until 1877. A comparable, if not superior, paper was developed by Crane & Co of Dalton, Massachusetts, a company that has supplied the paper for U.S. currency since 1885, although the linen content and the proportion of visible red or blue threads has been altered from time to time at the request of the U.S. Bureau of Engraving and Printing.

1857	Worldwide economic crisis.
1859	The world's first commercial oil well is drilled near Titusville, Pennsylvania.
1860	The Pony Express, a fast mail service by relays of pony riders, is established.
1861	The Civil War begins.
1863	President Lincoln issues the Emancipation Proclamation, Battle of Gettysburg.
1865	The Civil War ends, Lincoln is assassinated and the Ku Klux Klan is founded. The U.S. Secret Service is established. Its responsibilities and jurisdiction include detecting and arresting counterfeiters.
1866	First successful transatlantic cable is laid from Ireland to Newfoundland.
1867	The Alaskan Purchase.

Portrait of the Sioux chief Running Antelope

Why U.S. banknotes are green

The issue of U.S. Treasury paper money in 1861 sprang from the need to finance the Civil War, which had led to increased circulation of paper currency in both the Union and the Confederate states.

The Treasury was authorised by Congress to issue demand notes, which became better known as "greenbacks". Until the mid-nineteenth century all American paper money had been printed in black ink, combined with coloured tints as a deterrent against counterfeiting. But since even the early, primitive cameras could be used to produce bogus notes, a need arose for a coloured ink which, together with the black ink, could not be reproduced photographically. The rights for this patent green ink – first used in 1861 for greenbacks and Treasury notes – were acquired by Tracy R. Edson, one of the founders of the American Bank Note Company.

For technical reasons, the backs of the notes were printed in a darker shade than the green used on the faces, and the backs of the notes have been printed in green down to the present day. (Tradition has always been treated with profound respect by banknote producers.)

The shadow of Inflation

By the time the Civil War ended in 1865, the value of greenbacks in circulation had reached $450 million. Devaluation inevitably followed; a $100 note could be redeemed for only $75 in gold, a figure that later fell to $35. For the first time the depreciation of paper money, in itself no new phenomenon, was given a name: inflation.

Abraham Lincoln,
President of the United States from 1861 to 1865

1869	*Frank Lloyd Wright, perhaps the greatest American architect, is born at Richland Centre, Wisconsin.*
1875	*American Bankers Association is founded. Resumption Act orders specie payments to be resumed on 1 January 1879.*
1878	*Bland–Allison Act provides for the renewed coinage of silver dollars.*
1879	*Thomas A Edison perfects the first inexpensive incandescent light bulb.*
1880	*Herman Hollerith develops a tabulating machine with punched cards that revolutionises statistical techniques.*
1881	*The American humanitarian Clara Barton organises the American Red Cross.*
1883	*First skyscraper built in Chicago.*
1886	*Coca Cola marketed for the first time. Statue of Liberty erected in New York Harbour.*
1890	*National American Woman Suffrage Association founded.*
1897	*Hawaii annexed by the United States.*
1898	*Spanish–American War.*
1900	*Passage of the Gold Standard Act.*
1901	*President McKinley is assassinated.*
1906	*San Francisco is destroyed by earthquake and fire.*
1914	*Opening of the Panama Canal.*

Laundering Money

All banknotes, in time, wear out, and notes that have become unfit for use have to be sorted out and discarded – originally manually, but today by automatic sorting machines that can even identify counterfeits.

In 1909 the U.S. Bureau of Engraving and Printing noticed that at least 30 per cent of the notes returned by banks for destruction were not actually worn out but simply dirty. A curious episode in banknote history followed: the plan to wash and reissue soiled notes that were relatively well preserved, a process described as secondary banknote production.

By 1912, the Bureau had built a special currency laundering machine with which only two employees could wash, dry and iron up to 5,000 notes per hour. After a series of improvements, three machines were put into operation. During World War I, however, banknote paper changed: linen had become scarce, and cotton-based paper had to be used. But the new paper did not wash well: laundering altered the feel of the paper and the appearance of the notes, making it difficult to identify counterfeits. In 1918, the money-laundering programme was abandoned.

Banknote-washing machine

Symbolic figure "Panama", standing between two ships

303

$1 Silver certificate and Federal Reserve note

The face of the note carries a portrait of George Washington (1732–99), the first President of the United States of America (1789–97) and the father of his country. The portrait was engraved by George Frederick Cumming Smillie (1854–1924) after a painting of 1796 by Gilbert Stuart (1755–1828).

The motif on the back was first used for banknotes of the 1935 series and shows the two faces of the Great Seal of the United States, which was designed by William Barton and simplified by Charles Thompson, Secretary of Congress. It was adopted by Congress in 1782, and has remained unchanged ever since.

The face of the Seal shows an eagle, the breast of which has a shield with thirteen stripes. In its right talons, the bird holds an olive branch with thirteen leaves, symbolising peace, and in its left a bundle of thirteen arrows signifies the original colonies' fight for liberty; its head is turned towards the olive branch, indicating a desire for peace. A banner flying from the eagle's beak carries the Latin motto *"E pluribus unum"* ("One out of many") while over its head is a wreath of clouds containing thirteen stars. The words and symbols represent the original thirteen states.

On the reverse of the Seal is an unfinished pyramid, bearing at its base the Roman numerals MDCCLXXVI (1776), the year of the Declaration of Independence, and at its apex the eye of the all-seeing Deity in a triangular glory. Above the pyramid is the legend *"Annuit Coeptis"*, meaning "He [God] has favoured our undertakings" and below it are the words *"Novus ordo seclorum"*, or "A new order of the ages". Both inscriptions are quotations from Virgil's *Aeneid*.

Silver certificates were issued under the provisions of the legislation of 1878 and 1886, but have not been redeemable in silver since 24 June 1968, because of the rise in the price of silver. Most silver certificates bear a blue Treasury Seal, but some 1935A series notes issued during World War II for use in North Africa carry a yellow Treasury Seal.

Since 26 November 1963 the only $1 notes issued have been federal Reserve notes, with a green Treasury Seal.

1918	*President Wilson announces the "Fourteen Points" peace programme in a speech before Congress. Leonard Bernstein, conductor and composer, is born at Lawrence, Massachusetts.*
1919	*Ratification of the National Prohibition Amendment, prohibiting the manufacture, sale and transportation of alcoholic beverages in the United States.*
1920	*The Nineteenth Amendment gives American women the right to vote.*
1922	*Alexander Bell, inventor of the telephone, dies.*
1925	*Publication of Theodore Dreiser's novel* An American Tragedy.

$1 note of 1928, back

$1 note since 1935, showing the Great Seal of the United States

$2 United States note and Federal Reserve note

The portrait on the face of the note is of Thomas Jefferson (1743–1826), author of the Declaration of Independence, co-founder of the Democratic Party and the third President of the United States of America from 1801 to 1809; it was engraved by J. C. Benzing after a painting by Gilbert Stuart (1755–1828). The back of the older note shows a view of Jefferson's country house Monticello, which he designed himself – he was an architect, a musician and a lawyer as well as a statesman. Monticello is treasured by Americans as a national monument.

Federal Reserve Notes of the 1976 series were first circulated on 13 April 1976 (13 April is Jefferson's birthday) to commemorate the bicentennial of the Declaration of Independence. The face of the new note is unchanged; the back carries a motif showing the signing of the Declaration of Independence, taken from a painting by John Trumbull (1756–1843) which now hangs in the Trumbull Collection at the Yale University Art Gallery.

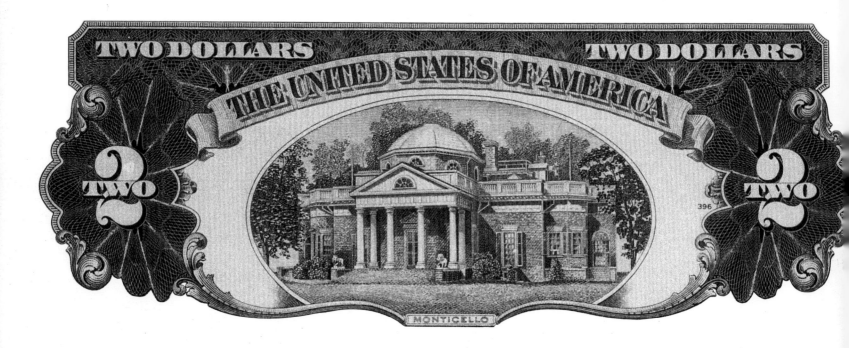

1927	Introduction of the first U.S. motion picture with sound. Non-stop solo flight from New York to Paris by Charles A. Lindbergh.
1929	"Black Friday": collapse of the New York stock market. The Great Depression begins.
1932	Tenth Olympic Summer Games held in Los Angeles; third Olympic Winter Games held in Lake Placid, New York. Franklin Delano Roosevelt takes office as President of the United States and launches the "New Deal".
1933	World's Fair in Chicago. High unemployment. The Gold Standard is abolished and the dollar devalued.

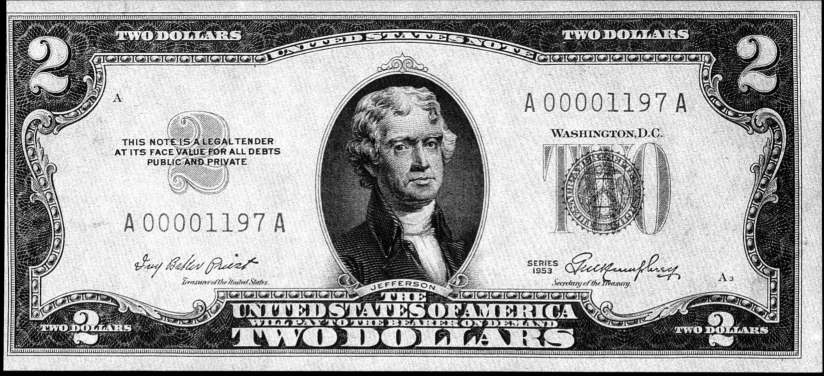

John Trumbull's painting "The Scene at the Signing of the Constitution"

$5 National Bank note

On the face of the note is the portrait of Abraham Lincoln (1809–65), Republican, the sixteenth President of the United States from 1861 to 1865, and the leader of the Union in the Civil War. He was assassinated shortly after his re-election had marked the success of his policy of reconciliation. The portrait was engraved by Charles Burt (1822–94) after a photograph taken in the studio of Mathew Brady on 9 February 1864.

The motif on the back is a view of the Lincoln Memorial in Washington DC, designed by the American architect Henry Bacon (1866–1924) in the style of a classic Greek temple, with the 36 columns of the exterior representing the 36 states of the union in 1865. The 19-foot-high statue of Lincoln was carved by the sculptor and medallist Daniel Chester French (1850–1931). Construction of the memorial began in 1917, and it was dedicated on 30 May 1922.

No portraits of the living

United States law today forbids the portrayal of any living person on a banknote or other official document of the United States of America. This was not always so: the portraits of President Abraham Lincoln and Secretary of the Treasury Salmon P. Chase appeared on notes in their own lifetime. But when the face of Spencer M. Clark, Chief Clerk of the National Currency Division of the U.S. Treasury, appeared on five cent fractional currency notes, during the Civil War, Congress Representative M. Russell Thayer of Pennsylvania proposed legislation to ensure that no one living could be so honoured again.

Legal tender note of 1862,
with the portrait of Salmon P. Chase,
Secretary of the Treasury from 1861 to 1864

$10 note of 1861,
with the portrait of President Lincoln

Photograph of Abraham Lincoln

$10 gold certificate

ORIGINAL HOME
1862 - 1880

HAMILTON

The face of the note carries a portrait of Alexander Hamilton, statesman, political economist and the first Secretary of the U.S. Treasury, holding office from 1789 to 1795; born in 1757, he met his end in a duel in 1804. It was engraved in 1906 by George Frederick Cumming Smillie after a likeness painted by John Trumbull (1756–1843). The reverse shows the U.S. Treasury building.

Gold certificates were notes that were convertible upon request into gold; they were identified by a yellow Treasury Seal under the Gold Reserve Act of 1933.

THE UNITED STATES OF AMERICA

10 TEN · 10 TEN
TEN DOLLARS
U.S. TREASURY

Gold $1 coin of 1858 obverse and reverse

TEN DOLLARS
IN GOLD COIN PAYABLE TO THE BEARER ON DEMAND

$20 Federal Reserve note

The portrait on this note is of Andrew Jackson (1767–1845), a popular military hero after the war of 1812 and nicknamed "Old Hickory" by his troops, Democrat, and seventh President of the United States from 1829 to 1837. It was engraved by Alfred Sealey in 1867 after a painting by Thomas Sully.

On the back is the White House in the Federal District of Washington DC, the official residence of the President of the United States since 1902. Designed by James Hoban in 1792, the mansion's bulk forms an architectural counterbalance to the massive Capitol building.

The White House, Washington DC

$50 note

Ulysses S. Grant (1822–85), Commander in Chief of the Union armies in the last stage of the Civil War, and champion of civil rights for black Americans, Republican and eighteenth President of the U.S.A. from 1869 to 1877, is shown on the front of the note. The portrait was engraved by Joseph Eissler.

On the back is the U.S. Capitol in Washington DC, where the Congress of the United States meets. Construction of this building, which was designed by William Thornton in late Georgian style, began in 1793. Under Jefferson's influence, classicism came to the fore in the early nineteenth century, and neo-classical elements were added to the building by Latrobe, who had taken over responsibility for its construction. It was completed by Thomas O. Walter, who added major extensions in the mid- nineteenth century and an iron dome in 1863.

Portrait of Ulysses S. Grant

$100 United States note

A portrait of Benjamin Franklin (1706–90), statesman and scientist, inventor, of (among other things) bifocal spectacles and lightning-rods, writer, publisher and master-printer, appears on the face of the note. Franklin was ambassador-at-large in London and Paris between 1757 and 1785 in order to further the cause of American independence. His portrait, like Grant's was engraved by Joseph Eissler.

The view shown on the back of the note is of Independence Hall, the former provincial State House of Pennsylvania, where the Second Continental Congress declared the colonies independent and the delegates signed the Declaration of Independence. In Independence Hall in 1781, Congress officially adopted the first instrument of the new United States Government – the Articles of Confederation. In the summer of 1787, a Federal Convention met in the State House Assembly Room and drafted the Constitution.

Portrait of Benjamin Franklin

$500 note

Eissler also engraved the portrait on the $500 note, that of William McKinley (1843–1901), champion of protectionism and twenty-fifth President of the United States from 1897 to September 1901, when he was shot dead by an anarchist at the Pan-American Exposition in Buffalo, New York.

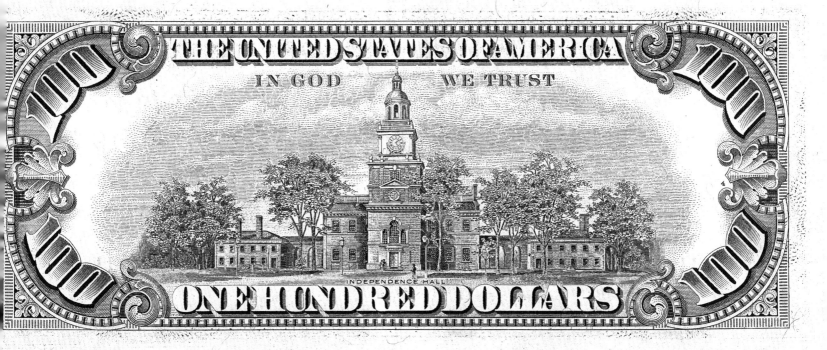

$1,000 note

Grover Cleveland (1837–1908) was the enemy of high tariffs and of public corruption, and the only President of the United States to serve two non-consecutive terms in office; he served as the twenty-second and twenty-fourth President, in 1885–89 and 1893–97 respectively. His portrait, again engraved by Joseph Eissler, appears on the face of the $1,000 note.

$5,000 note

The $5,000 note carries on the face a portrait of James Madison (1751–1836), the "father" of the U.S. Constitution, who became Jefferson's Secretary of State in 1801 and was the fourth President of the United States, in office from 1809 to 1817. The portrait was engraved by Alfred Sealey in 1869.

Portrait of James Madison, and "Washington resigning his commission", details from the $5,000 note of 1918

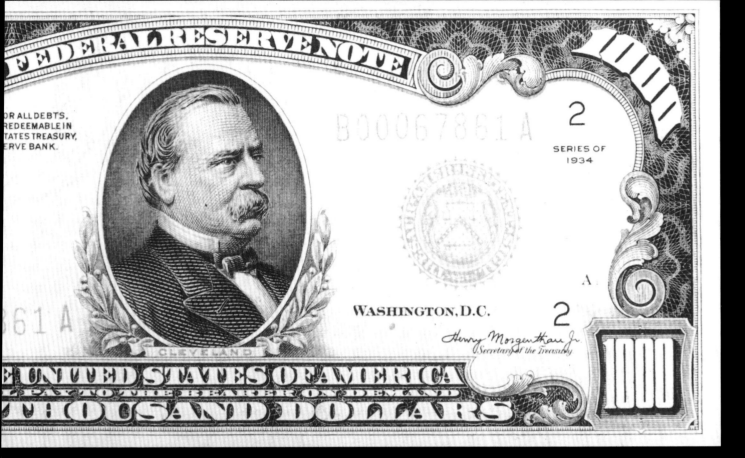

1934	Gold certificates can no longer be held by individuals.
1935	George Gallup starts the American Institute of Public Opinion.
1938	Munich Conference.
1941	Mount Rushmore National Memorial in South Dakota completed. Promulgation of the Atlantic Charter. Japanese attack on Pearl Harbour brings the U.S. into World War II.
1943	Roosevelt, Churchill and Stalin meet at Teheran
1944	Bretton Woods Conference establishes the U.S. dollar as the leading currency of the world. D-day: American, British and Free French troops land on the Normandy coast and begin the liberation of France.
1945	Foundation of the United Nations in San Francisco. United States planes drop nuclear bombs on Hiroshima and Nagasaki, ending World War II. The Nuclear Age begins.
1947	The Truman Doctrine breaches American isolationism.
1948	John Bardeen and Walter H Brattain invent the transistor. The Marshall Plan is launched, using American economic resources to stimulate the recovery of European economies.
1949	North Atlantic Treaty, signed by 12 nations, establishes the North Atlantic Treaty Organisation (NATO).
1950	Beginning of the Korean War.
1951	CBS begins limited television broadcasting in colour.
1952	Voice of America radio station starts broadcasting.
1953	Eugene O'Neill, American playwright, dies.
1955	J E Salk develops the first polio vaccine.
1957	The Civil Rights Act, a major landmark in Federal civil rights legislation, is passed.
1958	Foundation of the National Aeronautical and Space Administration (NASA). Nuclear submarine Nautilus pioneers the underwater passage to the North Pole.
1960	Development of the laser. Eighth Olympic Winter Games held in Squaw Valley, California.
1961	Ernest Hemingway, winner of the Nobel Prize for literature in 1954, dies.
1962	Cuban missile crisis. Communications satellite Telstar 1 launched.
1963	John F. Kennedy, 35th President of the United States, is shot dead in Dallas, Texas. "Hot line" set up between the U.S.S.R. and the U.S.A.
1965	Congress amends social security legislation to introduce "Medicare".
1966	"Black Power" movement.
1969	Neil Armstrong, American astronaut and commander of the lunar landing mission Apollo 11, is the first man on the moon. Ratification of the Nuclear Non-proliferation Treaty.
1971	Devaluation of the dollar, rise in the price of gold. Jazz trumpeter, singer and bandleader Louis Armstrong dies.
1972	President Nixon visits China. American swimmer Mark Spitz wins seven gold medals in the 1972 Olympics in Munich.

$10,000 note

The portrait of Salmon P. Chase, Secretary of the Treasury under President Lincoln from 1861 to 1864 and Chief Justice of the United States Supreme Court from 1864 to 1873, appears on the face of the $10,000 note. It was Chase who established a system of national bonds, and who authorised the use of the inscription "In God we trust" on United States coins. Under legislation passed in 1955, the motto now appears on all United States notes and coins.

$100,000 gold certificate

The $100,000 note is the highest denomination ever issued by the Bureau of Engraving and Printing; 42,000 of these notes were put into circulation. They were used for official transactions only and none ever circulated outside Federal Reserve Banks.

The note carries a portrait of Woodrow Wilson (1856–1924), the twenty-eighth President of the U.S.A. from 1913 to 1921, engraved by G. F. C. Smillie. Other parts of the design on the face of the note were engraved by O. Benzing and W. B. Wells, and the ornate decorations on the back by F. Pauling (all the notes of denominations of $500 and above carry elaborate designs featuring the denomination on their backs).

American notes issued since 1929

All American notes measure 156 by 66.3 mm, and are printed on high-grade creamy-white unwatermarked paper containing red and blue silk fibres. The intaglio printing on the faces of the notes is black, and the portraits and emblems on the backs are printed in green. The Treasury Seal, the serial number, the Federal Reserve Seal and the District number are overprinted by the letterpress process.

United States' paper currency comprises:

Federal Reserve notes
(notes of the Federal Reserve Banks with green Treasury Seal and serial number)

National Bank notes with brown Treasury Seal and serial number
(no longer printed)

United States notes with red Treasury Seal and serial number (no longer printed)

Silver certificates with blue Treasury Seal and serial number (no longer printed)

Gold certificates with yellow Treasury Seal and serial number (no longer printed).

The portraits carried on the faces of the notes and the emblems on the backs are shown opposite. The highest-denomination note issued at the time of writing is the $100 bill. Federal Reserve notes make up 99% of the paper money in public circulation in the United States today.

$1 bill: Washington   The Great Seal of the United States

$100 bill: Franklin   Independence Hall

$2 bill: Jefferson   The signing of the Declaration of Independence

$500 bill: McKinley

$5 bill: Lincoln   Lincoln Memorial

$1,000 bill: Cleveland

$10 bill: Hamilton   U.S. Treasury Building

$5,000 bill: Madison

$20 bill: Jackson   White House

$10,000 bill: Chase

$50 bill: Grant   U.S. Capitol

$100,000 bill: Wilson

AMERICAN NOTE-ISSUING INSTITUTIONS

Federal Reserve notes

In 1913 President Wilson initiated the "New Freedom programme" which, among other things, reorganised the banking and credit system and established a Federal Reserve System.

The programme divided the United States into twelve Federal Reserve Districts, with a Federal Reserve Bank in a major city in each District. Most of the Federal Reserve Banks also have branches in other large cities. Each District is designated by a number and the corresponding letter of the alphabet (1 = A, 2 = B, and so on).

The Federal Reserve Banks are empowered to issue currency with a symbol identifying the bank of issue. It is easy to tell which Federal Reserve Bank issued a particular note by looking at the Bank Seal, which is printed in black on the left of the portrait on the face of the note and carries the name of the Bank around its circumference; the letter corresponding to the District number stands in the centre of the Seal. The District number itself appears at the top and bottom of the face of the note, above and below the centre area just inside the engraved border. Moreover, the letter in front of the serial number – which appears in two places on the face of all United States currency – corresponds to that in the Bank Seal. The Treasury Seal and the serial number on the face of the note are printed in green.

For example, the Federal Reserve Bank of New York is the headquarters for the Second District. Notes issued by that Bank, therefore, carry the second letter of the alphabet, B, in the centre of the Bank Seal. The serial number has B as a prefix letter while the District number 2 appears at the top and bottom of the face of the note above and below the centre area just inside the engraved border.

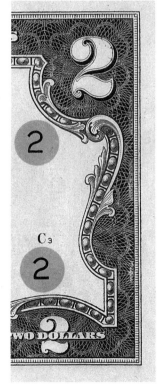

Federal Reserve notes are fully backed by collateral – either gold, Government securities, or high- grade, short-term commercial paper.

Towards the end of 1945, the printing of Federal Reserve notes in denominations of $500 and larger ceased, although the issue of the remaining supplies of these large denomination notes continued until 14 July 1969.

The District numbers, the cities in which the twelve Banks are located and the letter symbols are:

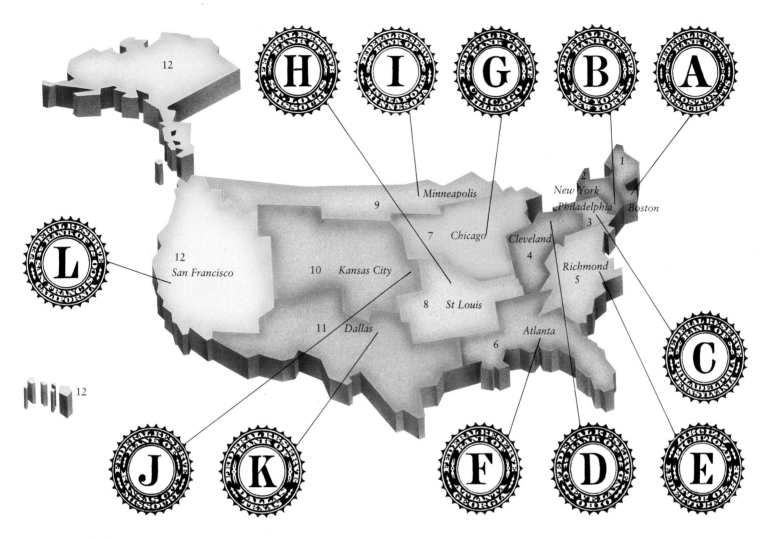

United States notes

United States notes, also called legal tender notes, have a history dating back to 1862, and were at one time issued in denominations ranging from $1 to $10,000; today, however, United States notes make up less than one per cent of the paper money in circulation The notes remain valid, and there is no plan to call in these or any other notes issued since 1861. All United States notes have a red Treasury Seal and serial number.

ACKNOWLEDGMENTS

The publishers are grateful to the following for permission to reproduce copyright material:

Picture	Credit
Eighteenth-century printing press	Technisches Museum für Industrie und Gewerbe, Vienna
Portrait of Sebastian Münster by Christoph Amberger	Bildarchiv Preußischer Kulturbesitz Photograph: Jörg P. Anders
Letter of 1816	Reproduced with the kind permission of the Mitchell Library, Sydney
20 Spanish dollars, 1824	Courtesy Westpac Banking Corporation Archives
City of London seen from Southwark, 1665	Copyright of the Museum of London
William of Orange, 1688	National Portrait Gallery, London
Detail of the Mint's Britannia	By courtesy of the Royal Mint
North West prospect of St Paul's Cathedral	Copyright of the Museum of London
Hargraves' Spinning Jenny	Trustees of the Science Museum, London
Crompton's Mule	Trustees of the Science Museum, London
Hackworth's "Royal George" locomotive, 1827 for Stockton and Darlington Railway	Trustees of the Science Museum, London
Wheatstone Printing Telegraph, 1841	Trustees of the Science Museum, London
The Penny Post, 6th May 1840	Post Office copyright
Vickers Vimy, Alcock and Brown's transatlantic aircraft, 1919	Reproduced by permission of Quadrant/FlightPicture
John Trumbull's painting showing the signing of The Declaration of Independence: "The Scene at the Signing of the Constitution"	United States Capitol Art Collection
Photograph of Abraham Lincoln	Collections of the Library of Congress

The Moneymakers International

first published in 1989 by
Black Bear Publishing Limited
King's Hedges Road
Cambridge CB4 2PQ
England

Designed by Peter Buchegger and Robert Kalina,
Oesterreichische Nationalbank, Vienna

Typeset by Black Bear Press Limited, Cambridge CB4 2PQ, England

British Library Cataloguing in Publication Data
The Moneymakers International
1. Banknotes . 1988
I. Kranister, W. (Willibald)
769.5'59

ISBN 0–9514522–0–7